Eliza Frances Pollard

Hope Deferred

Vol. 2

Eliza Frances Pollard

Hope Deferred
Vol. 2

ISBN/EAN: 9783337098582

Printed in Europe, USA, Canada, Australia, Japan

Cover: Foto ©Thomas Meinert / pixelio.de

More available books at **www.hansebooks.com**

HOPE DEFERRED.

BY

ELIZA F. POLLARD,

AUTHOR OF "AVICE," ETC.

IN THREE VOLUMES.
VOL. II.

LONDON:
HURST AND BLACKETT, PUBLISHERS,
13, GREAT MARLBOROUGH STREET.
1872.

PART II.

(CONTINUED.)

B

HOPE DEFERRED.

CHAPTER VI.

THE Count lay thus watching Jeanne as
one dreaming, only sometimes his eyes
would wander round the old familiar room
with a sad, hopeless look. He did not
speak, he did not seem to have the
power to do so. And Jeanne, her heart
was overflowing: words will not come when
the channels of the soul are too full. He
was there beside her—that was all she knew.
Dying! Her young strength, her love, re-
pudiated the idea. A strange sense of con-

tent was gradually creeping over her. Her love had come home at last, bruised, wounded, but still himself. She recognized him in each turn of the head, each movement of the hand. Each tone of the feeble voice awoke an echo in her heart, like a strain of music long unheard ; and a gladness diffused itself over her whole nature, dyeing her cheek a richer hue, lending a deeper brightness to her eyes.

After a time the Count seemed to revive. He roused himself from his apparent torpor. told Jeanne he thought he could eat now, and when they brought him a slice of cold chicken, tried to swallow it; but the effort was great, and the result small. Still, he was less intensely weary, and said, at last, quite suddenly,

" Jeanne, what have you been doing all these three years ?"

It was on her lips to ask him if he had not received any of their numerous letters; but she checked herself, saying only,

" Just the same as before you went away, Charles—seeing after the people, reading, riding, and painting."

" And you are not tired of the monotony, Jeanne ?"

" No," she answered ; then ventured to add, " But we have been very anxious about you. Why did you not write, Charles ?"

" Because I neither could nor would," he answered, eagerly, the light coming back to his eyes, and his voice gaining strength and power. " Listen to me, Jeanne ; it is best we should understand each other once for all. I have come home, I believe, to die. If I could blot out the last two years of my life, with all its acts and deeds, with all its memories, I would gladly do so; but, alas! I cannot, therefore, Jeanne, my cousin, let the dead bury their dead. Stand between me and the past; do not arouse it by word or question, do not let others do so. I left you a child, I come back to find you a woman, Jeanne; are you a generous one?"

"I cannot tell. What would you have me do?" she said, quietly.

"As I ask you, never to speak of the past, never to question me, and to make others understand that they must do the same. Will you be thus much my friend, Jeanne?"

She hesitated a minute; then said calmly,
" I will, Charles."

She was standing now beside him. Half
raising himself, half drawing her down towards him, he took her face between his
hands, and kissed her on the forehead, saying gently,

" Thank you, Jeanne, I will trust you.
When I am dead there will be no mystery."

Jeanne waited a few minutes longer; then,
taking up her shawl, said,

" I must go now, Charles. Mamma will
think I am lost. I will send Gordon
down."

" No, not to-night, Jeanne. I shall go
to bed; and Louis knows my wants better
than any one. Give my love to my aunt,

and tell her I would not send for her to-
night, for fear of frightening her. I shall
look less ill to-morrow morning. Good-
bye, my cousin." And he held her hand,
as if loth to let her go.

As Jeanne was leaving the house, accompanied by Jacqueline—for she had sent
Louis to his master—she met Gordon coming
to fetch her.

"Jeanne, what have you been doing all
the evening? We have grown quite anxious
at your long absence."

She put her arm in his, and bidding
Jacqueline good night, turned towards home.
A minute's silence, during which Gordon
perceived that something unusual had taken
place; then she said,

"Gordon, Charles de Lutz has come
home."

Had he been told that the Emperor of the French was at the Château de Lutz, Gordon would have been scarcely more surprised.

"Are you sure, Jeanne? Have you seen him?" he asked, standing still in his astonishment.

"I have been sitting with him for the last hour," answered Jeanne, quietly.

"Where is he, then?" asked Gordon. "Why did he not bring you back to the Cottage, instead of leaving Jacqueline to accompany you?"

"Because he is very ill, Gordon. He himself says he is dying. I do not quite think that. Still he is but the shadow of his former self."

"Then I will take you home, and go back to him," said Gordon.

"Nay, you must not do that," answered Jeanne. "His man Louis is with him. He is too worn-out to see any one to-night."

"Did he send for you, Jeanne?"

"No; he gave especial orders nobody was to be disturbed to-night; but Jacqueline was so terrified, when she saw how ill he was, that she, of her own accord, came up and told me. I could hardly believe her; and before alarming my mother thought I would ascertain the truth for myself."

"When did he arrive? And where does he come from?" asked Gordon.

"He arrived this evening," answered Jeanne. "I cannot tell you where he comes from," she continued, speaking slowly and distinctly, "for I have not questioned him, and shall not do so. Moreover, I have promised him that, as far as lies in my power, I will prevent other people doing so. He is very ill ; he says when he is dead the mystery of the last two years will be made clear. In the meantime, if he is to remain amongst us, they must be as a sealed book. Such are his words, and I do not see that we have any right to question them. He is accountable to no one."

"True, Jeanne," said Gordon, seriously ; " at least, so far as you and I are concerned at present ; but as regards your mother, I hold him somewhat responsible."

" I do not," answered Jeanne boldly. " Who ever dared to question the honour of a De Lutz ? I have passed my word to him that his wish shall be respected, and I think my mother will agree with me that it

ought to be. If he dies,"—her voice trembled as she gave utterance to the thought—
" we shall know all there is to be known ;
and if he lives, Charles de Lutz is not the
man to live under a cloud."

" It is well, Jeanne," answered Gordon.
" I have no right to demand an explanation
from the Count ; moreover, you know your
will is law with me. Am I not your vowed
knight?" And a smile, touching in its sadness, played round the young man's mouth.

" Thank you, Gordon," said Jeanne
gently. " And you will help me to silence
others also, will you not ?"

" I will do my best, Jeanne."

They had just reached the Cottage, and
were met at the entrance by Madame de
Lutz and Miss Ivor, the former saying,

"Jeanne, what have you been doing? Jacqueline should not have kept you out so late."

Jeanne did not answer at once, but throwing off her plaid, said,

"Mamma, I am very tired. Shall we go to bed? I can tell you what has detained me so long while I am undressing."

Jeanne's looks belied her words. There was no apparent fatigue in the glowing cheeks, the clear bright eyes, and the wakeful speaking happiness of mouth and lip; and as she turned to kiss and wish Miss Ivor good night, something of the merry, mischievous gladness of her early girlhood danced like a ray of sunshine on her sweet face.

"Ask Gordon to tell you what has happened, Amie; I must go to mamma," she whispered; and taking up the small bed-room lamp, which stood on the hall-table, she passed her arm lovingly round her mother's shoulders, and drew her into her own room.

As the door closed upon them, Miss Ivor turned to Gordon, saying,

"I am to ask you what has happened, Mr. Elliot."

"The Count de Lutz has returned," was the short answer.

"The Count returned!" exclaimed Miss Ivor, and she looked round as if she half expected to see him standing before her. "Where is he?"

"At the Château, I believe," answered Gordon,—"at least Jeanne says so."

"Then you have not seen him?"

"No. I would have gone and ascertained the fact for myself, but Jeanne objected. It seems he is very ill—he himself says dying; but Jeanne will not believe that. More than this I cannot tell you, Miss Ivor, except that Jeanne most earnestly begs that no questions may be asked. As regards the past, a strict silence is to be observed. Of course, as far as you or I are concerned, we have no right to question; but my aunt—I cannot but think she will be ill-satisfied. It is altogether an unsatisfactory state of affairs." He paused, and lifting his kindly, handsome face, looked straight into hers, saying in a lower voice, "Miss Ivor, why did Jeanne refuse the Count?"

"Because she did not wish to be his

wife—at least, I presume so," was the ready answer.

" Why not?" asked Gordon, thought-fully.

" Really I cannot tell you, Mr. Elliot," replied Miss Ivor. " Who can answer for a young girl's fancy? You know Jeanne was barely seventeen at the time."

" Yes, I know," said Gordon. " Do you think she has ever regretted her decision since, Miss Ivor?"

" I have never asked her, and never shall," was the quiet answer; " and if I were you, I would not allow it to occupy my thoughts too much, Mr. Elliot—it will scarcely conduce to your happiness."

" I daresay you are right," said Gordon, sighing heavily. " Good night, Miss Ivor."

She held out her hand.

"Good night, Mr. Elliot. Instead of Rome, why do you not go to Switzerland?"

"You recommend mountain air?" he asked, with the shadow of a smile.

"I recommend anything that is bracing," she answered. "Believe me, it is not good to dream—one's head gets full of fancies—fancies which we laugh at a few years later."

"May be, when they are fancies," said Gordon, seriously.

"Which is more often the case than we imagine, or are willing to believe. Take my advice, and go to Switzerland. Now, good night." And, shaking him heartily by the hand, she left him still standing in the door.

"Poor fellow!" she murmured, closing her own door; "one heart healed, another bleeding. How will it all end?" And, throwing herself into her arm-chair, she sat thinking till a late hour, strange misgivings filling her mind for the future of the pupil she loved so well.

Jeanne, closeted alone with her mother, told her gently all that had passed—how Charles de Lutz had come home ostensibly to die. "But, mamma dear, I do not think he will—a little good nursing, a little care, and he will be well again," she said. "And then, doubtless, he will tell us the secret of the last two years. In the meantime we must be patient, and not drive him away again. Is it not so, mother mine?"

And Madame de Lutz could but agree

with her, promising to respect for the time, at least, the sick man's request. She was so thankful to have him back again, she would have acceded to far more difficult terms.

And so the night closed over the sleeping inmates of the Château and the Cottage. Sleeping, did I say?—there was little sleep for one fair girl, who lay beneath the white curtains of her bed, with eyes wide open, waiting for the dawn of day, fearful lest the rising sun should disperse her new-found happiness.

CHAPTER VII.

IT was still early, and the household at the Cottage was hardly stirring when Jacqueline made her appearance, bathed in tears, and informed the astonished servants of the Count's arrival on the previous evening.

"But he is dying, I tell you," said Jacqueline. "To think of his coming home in this state! He has poisoned himself with paints—that is what he has done. Oh! my God! my God!" and she wrung her hands. The woman loved both the Count and Jeanne beyond all things else. The Count had been her foster-child, and Jeanne her nursling, therefore her grief was by no means exaggerated. "Some one must go over at once to Amonville, and bring Monsieur Auber back," she continued. "I thought we should never have got him through the night. He is just sinking."

The servants looked at each other, scarcely knowing whether to believe Jacqueline or not, the news was so perfectly unexpected.

"Does the Countess know?" asked the coachman.

"Doubtless, Mademoiselle Jeanne must have told her. Robert, I say you must saddle the fleetest horse you have—there is no time to lose."

" Very well," answered the man. " Mind,
if you have been dreaming, Jacqueline, you
will bear the blame."

" I am not given to trouble folk with my
dreams, or else you would have had little
peace for the last month," answered Jacqueline, sharply. " When I saw my blessed
Count carried into his own Château last
night more dead than alive, I was no more
surprised than if one of you had walked in.
I knew he was in a bad way. Have I not
seen him laid out as a corpse three nights
running? Ah! well, I have no time to tell
you all that now, but I knew mischief was
brewing. Why must he needs go to Italy
and poison himself with paints, as if there
were not enough in France?" And she
began whimpering afresh.

"Now, Jacqueline, what's the use of crying?" said Robert. "If the Count is really here, and ill, we must all put our shoulders to the wheel and get him well again. We can't afford to lose him. There was not a better master in the whole province, and we have missed him sorely. I'll be off to Amonville as quickly as Mademoiselle's mare will carry me, and you go and wake the young lady, and tell her how bad the master is."

And with that the coachman, who had been in the family from earliest boyhood, left the kitchen, and Jacqueline went to Jeanne's room. She knocked gently, not to awake Madame in the next apartment. Jeanne opened the door immediately. She was already more than half dressed.

"What is it, Jacqueline?" she asked, fearfully.

"The Count has been as bad as he could be all night, Mademoiselle, and I have just sent Robert off to Amonville to fetch Mr. Auber."

"Is he really so ill as that, Jacqueline? I thought last night it was more fatigue than anything else."

"Ay, fatigue of the worst sort, Mam'selle Jeanne. He has just no more strength in him than a babe. It seems those Italian doctors have been bleeding and blistering his very life away. At least, so Louis says."

"Ah! Jacqueline," said Jeanne, passing her hand across her brow, as if to clear away a dark mist. Then she spoke quickly,

"Go to Mr. Elliot's room, wake him, and ask him, from me, to go down to the Château and remain with the Count until my mother can join him. He ought not to be alone with Louis."

"No, Mam'selle, indeed he ought not. Louis is as good as he can be, and knows his master's ways; but when a man is as ill as Count Charles, his own people ought to be with him."

"Very well, Jacqueline; go quickly."

The woman obeyed; and Jeanne, closing the door of her room, threw herself on her knees and prayed—prayed with all the passion of a woman suing for the life of the man she loved. She did not weep—tears do not come in moments such as these. "Ask and it shall be given you." And

Jeanne asked in perfect faith, in full confidence, never doubting, "My God, grant me this man's life. Take from me what Thou wilt, but spare—spare him to my love!"

Straight to the throne of God such prayers ascend, borne on the wings of faith. Strengthened and calmed, Jeanne rose, and passed into her mother's room. In less than an hour Madame de Lutz was standing beside her nephew's bedside—his death-bed, she thought, when she first set eyes upon his altered face. He had scarcely strength left to lift his head, with something of his old courteous grace, as his aunt bent over him, tears, which she strove in vain to check, trickling down her face. He suffered no actual pain; only the weariness, the exhaustion was intense, and the complete prostration of that once noble form was terrible to see.

Mr. Auber's visit did not tend to encourage them.

" He is suffering from the effects of the worst sort of low typhus fever. I doubt if he will ever be the same man again," said the doctor, " even suppose he ultimately recovers. How he has managed to travel is more than I can tell; and, of course, the re-action is terrible. He has not much fever now; but he is sinking from exhaustion. I scarcely think his constitution can bear up against the shock. I would warn you also, Madame, against allowing Mademoiselle to see her cousin. In its present stage the fever is still infectious, and she could not bear up against it."

" But she saw him before any of us,"
answered Madame. " The mischief is done
already."

" Perhaps not," answered the doctor.
" In any case, she is best out of his room—
she can do no good there."

And so Jeanne was banished ; and Madame de Lutz, Jacqueline, and Louis divided the watching. Gordon, notwithstanding considerable opposition on his part,
shared Jeanne's banishment.

Days passed by, bringing little or no
change. Sometimes Madame's heart would
sink to the lowest ebb. " There is no
vitality in him—he does not try to live," she
would say to Jeanne and Miss Ivor ; " and
all I can get out of Louis is, ' He has been
worse, Madame, far worse.' "

But though others despaired, Jeanne never did.

" He will live, mother—I feel sure he will," she would say, cheeringly, when, worn out with care and watching, she sought rest and comfort in her daughter's company.

Once made aware of her presence, the Count could not bear his aunt out of his sight.

The first day he had asked for Jeanne, but when told of the doctor's prohibition, he had acquiesced directly, saying, as he turned wearily on the pillow,

" God knows I would not bring harm to her. Enough have suffered already."

" When we are tired, she will be fresh," Madame de Lutz had said. " Gordon,

0123456
7890

12 34567890123

45 Jeanne, and Miss Ivor will be your conva-
lescent nurses."

Alas! convalescence did not seem to come
quickly.

And Jeanne, what did she do through
those weary hours of watching and of waiting? Her heart, her thoughts in the sick-
chamber, yet forced to keep a calm exterior,
and not venturing, in her maidenly reserve,
to murmur at the decree which forbade her
active service. She was learning her lesson
of womanly patience and endurance. He
who knoweth all things knew how she
would need it, and, like a tender father, was
gradually and gently moulding her to her
lot.

It was as well for everyone that Jeanne
had no especial tie to bind her, for she was

enabled to minister to the comfort of invalid and nurses far more than she guessed herself, her ready wit and thoughtful care supplying all deficiencies. Nothing passed into the Count's room but what Jeanne first saw and approved. There was no haste, no disorder in the household. The meals were carefully served at the usual hours, and, if possible, more than habitual care was bestowed upon those little details of household economy which tend so much to the comfort and rest of those concerned, and which, at the appearance of sickness in a house, so often entirely disappear, thereby increasing the fatigue of the watchers, and naturally, however careful one may be, to a certain extent affecting the sufferer.

And Jeanne's hope—let us call it by a

higher name, "her faith,"—never failed.
She moved like a ministering spirit about
the Château, cheering everyone who crossed
her path with her sweet smile and gentle,
kindly words.

"She is like a ray of sunshine," Louis
said one day to Jacqueline. "It does one's
heart good to look at her. I never thought
Mam'selle Jeanne beautiful before."

"Then it must have been wilful blindness," answered Jacqueline, crossly. "Your
travelling has served, at least, to open your
eyes; let us hope it may do the same by the
master, and that he will settle down quietly
now among his own people, and marry
Mam'selle. He may look for and not find
a better or a fairer Countess."

"Ah! Jacqueline, he should have done

that three years ago," answered Louis, sadly, "it is too late now." And therewith he went about his business.

This was more than Louis had ever ventured to say before. He was usually perfectly silent as to everything concerning his master.

And Jeanne watched and prayed. The villagers would tell, long afterwards, how, morning and evening, she might be seen in the village church praying. Day after day she came, kneeling before no especial altar, but bowing her head low in prayer and supplication before the God and Saviour of the world. He who knew the most secret emotions of her woman's heart, who loved and blessed the little children, to Him Jeanne came fearlessly, and asked

the life of him whom, next to God, she
loved. And the peasant women, sitting at
their cottage doors, would see her pass, and
as she disappeared beneath the porch would
silently follow her, some carrying infants in
their arms, others with children clinging to
their gowns, and kneeling down, they, too,
would pray after their fashion, muttering
over and over on their chaplets a " Pater
Noster" and an " Ave Maria." It was an
act of kindly faith, and comforted Jeanne's
heart.

Nobody knew exactly when the Count
first began to mend. It was so gradual as
not to be reckoned by days, but weeks.
Still he did improve ; and, at last, one day
finding himself alone in his room, something of his old energy came back to him,

and he crept to the *atelier*.   Jeanne was there, sitting on a low chair by the window, working.   She started up as the door opened, and in another moment was at the Count's side.

"Is this prudent? Have you done well?" she asked, trying to steady her voice, for the suddenness of his appearance had un-nerved her.

"I think so, Jeannette, as I have been able to do it," he answered, smiling, and laying his hand on her shoulder to support himself. And Jeanne, as she guided him to an arm-chair, knew that her prayer was granted—that Charles de Lutz would not die! His voice was clear and full—no longer hopelessly weary, as when it fell upon her ear the night of his return. Only, as Jeanne looked at him, she saw that the sadness had not left his eyes; alas! it was too deep-seated. So she talked to him and cheered him, till the genial smile came back to mouth and lip, and unwittingly he found himself teasing and order·ing her about as in former days. Still the shadow rested on him, and not even Jeanne, with all her tact and brightness, had power to disperse the gloom.

When Madame de Lutz returned, and, not finding the Count in his own room, repaired to the *atelier*, and saw how matters stood, he was inexpressibly relieved. It was the lack of all willingness or desire to exert himself which had so tried both her and the doctor. He had said he had come home to die, and the idea was so fixed in his mind that it was only by slow and difficult degrees that he had allowed the possibility that he might recover.

" Aunt," he said, holding out his hand to her, "you must forgive me. I have raised the quarantine. I do not think Jeanne will take any harm now."

" I am heartily glad you have taken the matter into your own hands," answered Madame, cheerfully. "I have long thought the precaution useless; but I did not like openly to disobey the doctor. You already look better for the change."

" Do I ?" he answered. " I have been telling Jeanne half my illness has been caused by the shock she gave my nerves the night of my return. I expected to see my pretty, sunny little Cousin Jeanne, and I found a stately young lady. What shall I do for a plaything, aunt?"

Scarcely had the words passed his lips when a thought, agonizing in its intensity, seemed to cross his brain. His face turned deathly pale, and, closing his eyes, he let his head fall back upon the pillows.

"I do not think you much need a play-fellow at present," said Madame de Lutz, as she hastened to bathe his brow with eau de Cologne.

"True, aunt," he rejoined, a minute after-wards—"I forgot myself. Life has nothing left for me but stern reality."

CHAPTER VIII.

"NO sterner for you than for other men, Charles," said Madame de Lutz, looking steadily at the Count; and, going up to him, she continued, gently, "I know nothing of your life for the last two years; and until you choose to break the silence, no man or woman has a right to question you. Were I your mother, I would not do it. Confidence, to be real, must be freely given. Therefore the past will be as a dead letter until you yourself break the seal.

But, Charles, now there is work for you to do, work which has been calling for you, and which no other hand but your own can worthily accomplish. Your life has been spared, and I entreat you, for the honour of your house and of your name, to take up once more the broken threads of that life, and to make the end worthy of the beginning."

Charles de Lutz was silent—he never was a man of many words; and, feeling deeply, said but little. The silence therefore which followed Madame de Lutz's words might have been awkward, had it not been broken by the deep, full organ tones pealing forth one of Beethoven's melodies, soul-quieting, soul-searching, filling the room, and driving all idle thought away—now soft and low, then rising in full harmony of touch and sound.

No unpractised hand was Jeanne's. Some might have thought she lacked brilliancy; but there was power in her music—the power of the soul. Each note she played told its own tale, and was its own interpreter. And as Charles de Lutz lay and listened to her, with his aunt's last words still ringing in his ears, the mist seemed clearing away from brain and heart. Steadily he looked back upon the past, whatever that past might be; earnestly, courageously, he gazed forward into the future. All that through those long months of sickness, when body and soul were alike diseased, had seemed difficult, if not impossible, to compass, grew now comparatively easy of

accomplishment—at least possible, worthy of
the effort. He seemed to see the road along
which he had to walk, and though stones
and barriers might lie across his path and
impede his progress, he felt no longer power-
less to combat, maybe to overthrow them.
The burden of his past life, wrong or right,
he knew that he must still bear ; but at that
moment, in the quiet stillness of that old
room, with music stealing over his whole
being, and the familiar forms of his almost
mother and his sister-friend beside him,
courage and life seemed to come back together. He knew that he should live, and
he almost marvelled to think how he had
courted death.

Long Jeanne played—until the growing
shadows warned her that evening was draw-

ing in, and that it was hardly prudent for an invalid to be still seated at the open window; so she stopped her playing, and, rising, closed the casement. In so doing she passed by her cousin. He held out his hand, and, taking hers, said,

" Thank you, Jeanne. I understand now how David dispelled Saul's evil spirit."

His brow was clear, his voice had the old familiar ring of strength and power. A thrill of gladness ran through Jeanne's frame, as she answered softly,

" We all need, or perhaps imagine that we need, a David at some period of our lives." And smiling pleasantly upon him, she went her way.

That same evening, for the first time since the Count's return, the whole party, namely,

Madame, Gordon, Jeanne, and Miss Ivor, assembled in the studio, with the Count in their midst, and once more the home-life seemed to begin afresh. Her twenty-one years rested lightly on Jeanne. How joyous she was that night, how sunny her smile, how soft and musical her laugh; how womanly and graceful the attitude of form and face as she bent over her embroidery-frame, ever and anon tossing back her head, and brushing away with her hand the hair that fell in soft waves upon her brow—an old trick, familiar to her from childhood, and which Charles de Lutz smiled at as he recognized it once more.

This was the first step towards recovery, and from henceforth the progress was rapid. No sooner was it generally known that the

Count was beginning to get about than visits and congratulations poured in. Among the very first was Madame la Marquise de la Croix.

Jeanne and her mother received the guests, and answered all inquiries; but after the first week or so people began to ask for the Count himself, and to marvel at his non-appearance. Gently Madame de Lutz hinted the same to her nephew, and gently, but decisively, received for answer,

" Aunt, I have come back, but not to mix in the world ; that, for the present, at least, is over. I will live now for my people, and by-and-by, when I have the strength, for my art—into society I will not go. I have no taste, no inclination for it. Nor will I receive guests in my own house, save those few old friends who will come without form or ceremony; but balls and fêtes, and all the various calls of society, I will not respond to."

"Then you mean to live a hermit's life, Charles?" said his aunt.

He looked at her. A clear, earnest smile lighted up his whole face.

"I trust you will have no reason to ask me that question six months hence, aunt. You told me the other day that there were neglected duties of two years' standing awaiting me. I am going to find them out and accomplish them now. I do not think I shall have much idle time; and do not fear for me, aunt, I shall be a nine-days' wonder, and then the good people of Amonville will have forgotten my existence, or, if they do think of me, it will be as an eccentric individual, unworthy of their favours."

Madame de Lutz shook her head, but was satisfied by the tone of the answer. At the Cottage they had lived so quietly for the last two or three years, that the sudden influx of visitors had rather disturbed them than otherwise, and they were glad once more to subside into their own home-life.

Steadily and earnestly the Count went to work. Long before he was able to go about and freely mix with his people, he learnt from Jeanne all that most intimately concerned both them and the estate. She knew everything, was familiar with every family, knew each birth, each marriage on the estate; not a sorrow nor a joy for miles round but what she shared it; not a cottage-roof needing repairs but what she was cognizant of the fact. Unpaid rents, neglected work, and ill-kept farms, she could point out, one and all; and she did so now, so clearly and distinctly that, while still confined to the house, the Count regulated many things, with the out-door assistance of Gordon and his bailiff; receiving also his chief tenants, hearing and redressing complaints. He had ever been a clement landlord, but he was now more especially so, passing over many things which he would not formerly have allowed, saying simply, "It is my fault. Had I been present such and such a thing would not have happened." Only he told his people that he hoped from henceforth to live among them, that their interests would be mutual, and that he should expect each and all to do their duty to him, even as he should strive to do his by them.

The first active use he made of his returning strength was to drive over to Amonville. On this expedition he refused all company save that of his valet Louis. He was absent nearly the whole day, and on his return shut himself up in his own room on plea of business. The following morning the old family lawyer arrived at the Château, and was closeted with the Count for several hours. Later, when the old man went to pay his respects to Madame de Lutz, his face was serious almost to sadness, but she was too delicate to demand, and he too discreet to offer, an explanation.

The day after this interview Louis started

for Italy, to pack and forward to Lutz all that remained there of his master's possessions. The Count's return had been so hurried, and under such unfavourable circumstances, that much had been left behind. Charles de Lutz was restless, and evidently anxious, for the first week or ten days after Louis was gone; but upon the receipt of certain papers he grew calmer, and gradually threw himself once more heart and soul into the life he had cut out for himself. With health came renewed energy, too much perhaps—it was a reaction. With almost feverish hands he laboured now; but the brightness, the easy, careless brightness, which had so marked his artist nature, never came back again; or, if it did, only in faint gleams. In the midst of merry talk or gay repartee, a shadow would settle on his face, extinguishing the light in his eye, and, like a wintry ray of sunshine, the smile would die out on brow and lip. There was no mistaking it; however much he might try to hide it, Charles de Lutz was a saddened man, a cloud had overshadowed his life—it remained to be seen how long the silver lining would be hidden from view. And in the meantime, with Jeanne at his side, he worked hard to make up for lost time. Nobly and efficaciously they laboured; she, with her perfect knowledge, and her woman's heart, which made her the beloved, the angel of every household; he, using his authority, soon re-established order, and be-

fore the Autumn had well set in the inhabitants of Lutz rejoiced in having once again
found their master.

Ere this Gordon Elliot had returned to
England. Towards the end of the long
vacation, when the Count was fairly on the
road to convalescence, he had bidden them all
farewell, joined some fellow-students in
Switzerland, and from thence gone back to
Oxford, to keep his last term. Miss Ivor,
too, had absented herself on a visit to some
old friends in Paris, and the two cousins,
and Madame de Lutz, found themselves alone,
as in Jeanne's childhood. So the Count and
Jeanne rode and walked, worked and
painted together. Painted, did I say?
Jeanne painted, and the Count looked on,
but never touched a brush.

"I cannot, Jeanne, I cannot yet awhile —it will come in time."

This he had said one day when she had urged him to paint. She never did so again —she saw it hurt him in no common way. Indeed, all sedentary employment seemed to tell upon and harass him greatly. Thus by degrees all business correspondence, the looking over and settling of accounts, fell into Jeanne's hands. It happened thus. One night he arrived at the Cottage, tired and worn out with some difficult business, and with a long day's ride in bad weather right across the country. He brought with him some accounts to verify, and business letters to read and answer. He was weary both in mind and body, utterly unfitted for the task. Madame interfered, telling him he was wrong, very wrong, and would only make himself ill again. That night he desisted to please her, but the following evening he did not return, and Jeanne learnt from old Jacqueline that he had passed the greater part of the night in the study at work. So the next evening the writing-table was prepared, and Jeanne, turning laughingly to him, said,

"Now, Charles, you may dictate, and I will write; you may listen, and I will read. Try me for your secretary, just for one week —then, if you are not satisfied, dismiss me."

And so the partition of labour was accepted, somewhat unwillingly at first, on the Count's part, but he soon found he had no reason to regret it.

"Let her try, Charles," Madame had said. "Sooner or later she will have to manage her own estate. It is well she should learn."

And Jeanne's head was as sound as her heart—it only needed a little guidance, a little tempering. Steadily she went to work—timidly at first, but determined to succeed. Was it not for him she worked? How, then, could she fail? And she did not. From henceforth the Count and she together managed the whole estate, in the day time abroad, and at night at home. When their task was done, those three would gather round the fire, the table drawn in front of the hearth, laden with bright china, and the hissing silver urn, behind which Jeanne took her place; and then would ensue that pleasant idle converse which only grows with close familiarity. Sometimes, but not often, the Count would tell of his sojourn in Italy; but he rarely spoke of himself, or of events of personal interest. It was not his own life he told, but that of those with whom he had mixed, or who had casually crossed his path. Both Madame de Lutz and Jeanne noticed this—they could not fail but do so, yet they kept silence, even to each other—the time for speaking had not come yet; they were waiting, waiting!

So, calmly, and without interruption, the Winter months passed by. And Jeanne, was she happy? Yes, indeed she was! Is the sailor happy when he comes within sight of port? So was Jeanne happy, quietly, serenely, working with and for the man she loved. Seeing him each day, hearing his voice, sunning herself in his companionship. The two thrown together, united by common interests and occupations, grew together; their tastes and their opinions meeting, developing, they learnt to know each other as man and woman, no longer man and child. They stood on an equality, he governing and guiding, she suggesting, helping, sympathizing, ever tender and true, lending a grace to the rudest task, each supplying what the other lacked—only complete together.

And Jeanne was glad, right glad, looking neither before nor behind, content to live in and for the present. Was it not joy enough for her to know, when she awoke in the morning, that before many hours she should be at his side, that she had work to do for him ; to know that his face would brighten at her coming; to know that she alone had power to clear the cloud away from his brow ? Ay, surely that was joy enough ! And if at times a certain sense of incompleteness crept over her, she cast it from her, she would not pause long enough to recognize the void. Had she not her life to live, her work to do? Something had bruised and wounded him she loved, him whom she had sent from her, though she loved him, and because she loved him.

Never once did Jeanne regret her past conduct. She knew now better than ever how terrible a loveless life with him would have been to her, how soul and body would alike have suffered. She knew it better now than in her girlish days, because she understood better. Then love had been but a dream, a tenderness, a something undefined; now it was the ruling passion of her life, a component part of herself. To know that she was his, that he was hers; to have no thought apart, no dream in earth or heaven in which he did not mingle; to follow in his footsteps, to hold his hand through life's long journey, never to part, never to weary; to let the whole world run its course, so that they two stood together, and nought came between them; to love and to be loved! Such was Jeanne's dream.

And gradually creeping over her came the knowledge that she did not love alone.

Timidly, fearfully, she recognized the fact.
Yet in no way did it alter her. He never
spoke to her of love; he never sought to
win her. She was outwardly, to all intents,
the sister friend she had ever been; and she
was content to wait. Nothing could change
her; she had loved, she did love, and she
should ever love him—just as she believed
in God above.

Thus she lived on from day to day. And
he who was the object of this pure devotion
knew not, dreamt not of its existence; had
he known, he would have fled for dear
life away. But with such gentle maidenly
reserve, such quiet self-possession, did Jeanne
accomplish her daily tasks, easing his burdens, cheering his solitude, that her very
simplicity of word and deed was a bar

against any thought of passion, even had he been so inclined. He knew that she was supremely necessary to him, but he never asked himself why her presence filled the aching void, and stilled the agonizing pain ever gnawing at his heart; he did not even recognize the fact that it *was* her presence. She was ever there, ever willing, ever ready. Twice she had refused to be his wife; truly no thought of danger for him or her presented itself to his mind.

But there was a looker-on who soon saw with her mother's eye the course events were likely to take. Earlier, Madame de Lutz would have rejoiced deeply at the affection she saw growing from day to day, the very thing she had deemed impossible, the love she had so coveted for Jeanne, coming, coming, like the rising tide; she heard the murmur of the waves in the distance, and her heart trembled. Woman that she was, she knew the signs. She remembered how her own lover had learnt unwittingly to need and seek her—how wistfully his eye had wandered round the room until it rested upon her—how soft his voice had grown when speaking to her —how tender the touch of his hand! All these signs she saw now for the first time in Charles de Lutz, and with the mystery of the last two years hanging over him, she feared and trembled.

One early Spring morning, the inhabitants of the Cottage were waiting in the boudoir for breakfast to be announced. Miss Ivor had returned, and the Count was there, as usual. The village postman had just brought up the letters, which had been duly distributed. Jeanne was standing at the open window reading hers. Turning quickly round, she gave it to her mother, saying simply,

"I think I ought to go, mamma."

"I think so too," answered her mother, after perusing the note; and without further remark, she once more turned to her own letters.

"Where ought you to go, Jeanne?" asked the Count, coming and standing beside her.

"To Amonville," answered Jeanne. "Madame Beauvais gives a party to-morrow, and she has sent me a most pressing invitation. However, that does not constitute the 'ought.' It encloses a note from Clo-

tilde, which seems to intimate that the
party is only an excuse—that once more
she has been asked in marriage, and this
time she must make up her mind either to
matrimony or the convent. She is to see
the gentleman at the ball to-morrow night.
I think she will choose the convent."

" Why, Jeanne ?"

" Because Clotilde is good and true,
Charles, and cannot make up her mind to
falsehood. The Beauvais are fairly well
off, but there are three daughters, and
though not noble, their father expects them
to marry well. The men he presents to
them are not likely to fix their affections ;
young men do not suit ; their positions are
not made ; his daughters must have estab-
lishments, and so Clotilde has vexed him

more than once by refusing to marry. She is now five-and-twenty—old for a French girl; and her younger sisters are women, too, and, moreover, wild to get married, and they openly declare it is her fault they are not settled—that men are afraid of a family of three girls; so she has no very cheerful life between them all, and I think the end is coming."

Breakfast was here announced, and as they passed into the dining-room, the Count said,

"Shall I drive you into Amonville to-morrow, Jeanne?"

"Thank you, I should have liked it, but Clotilde writes that she will be paying some visits in the neighbourhood of Lutz this afternoon, and that she will stop at the Cottage, dine with us, and then we can drive back to Amonville together this evening."

"To talk over the new proposal?" said the Count, smiling.

"Even so," said Jeanne; "but I shall certainly not advise her to marry a man she cannot love."

"You would rather choose the convent, Jeanne?"

"Happily that will not be my alternative," she answered. "I have my mother and my home. Poor Clotilde!" And gathering round the breakfast-table, the conversation ceased.

Early in the afternoon Jeanne heard the Count order his horse, and shortly afterwards he came into the boudoir where she was working with Miss Ivor.

" Good-bye, Jeanne," he said, holding out his hand. " If you go to Amonville this afternoon I shall not see you again. Take care of yourself."

"Shall you not be home to dinner?" asked Jeanne.

" No ; I have business at Bauri. You will leave the key of the secretary, so that I may look over those leases to-morrow."

" Yes, I will give it to mamma," she answered ; and, shaking hands, they parted.

Jeanne's cheek almost paled as she heard the last tramp of his horse's feet. She should not see him for three days! Three days! She marvelled to herself how they would pass! His absenting himself did not surprise her. He never stayed at the Cottage when there were visitors ; but it was

just that which grieved her. Would he
always be thus ? Would the social brightness of former days never come back to him?
His glory, his ambition, his art, all faded
away in their first freshness! She could
have wept at the thought; but within her
rose the gladness, the power of her own
youth, that hopefulness which was her
great characteristic ; and she thought of the
future growing out of the past, the clouds
dispersed, only the blue sky overhead. And
thus smiling to herself, she once more
dreamt her dream of regenerating love.
Oh ! blindness of woman's heart ! We think
we know, we think we see, and all the
while love and our own desires cast their veil
over our eyes.

A carriage rolling up the drive roused her,

and a minute afterwards Clotilde and her
sister Marie entered the room. Jeanne
sprang forward to meet them with joyous
welcome.

" You will come to the ball, will you not.
Jeanne?" were Clotilde's first words; adding, "Mamma delayed asking you to the
very last, and only then did so at my earnest
entreaty. She said it was no use, you always refused. But you will come home
with me to-day, dear, will you not? I
want you." And as she spoke she held
Jeanne's hand in hers, and looked up into
her face, her dark eyes speaking volumes.

" Indeed I will," answered Jeanne, kissing her. " It was settled I should go as
soon as I received your letter this morning."

"Ah! you ought to have had it sooner," said Clotilde, quickly; "but all the invitations went out late, and yours last of all. Mamma said it was a mere form, but I knew I could persuade you."

Clotilde Beauvais had never been beautiful, barely pretty; but hers was a good face, frank and open, her look fearlessly true. As a young girl she had been somewhat brusque in manner and in speech, but that had softened down of late, and a certain sadness had taken the place of her youthful spirits. She was not the favourite daughter with either father or mother; and from her girlhood she had felt herself in the way, especially since her sisters had become marriageable, and she had the misfortune to refuse two or three offers, utterly distasteful to her in every way. Then she was told that she was neglecting her duty, standing in the light of her younger sisters, who made her daily feel how unreasonable her conduct seemed to them, thus preventing their establishment in life. And the mother, in her turn, sighed.

"If I had only two daughters to take into society!—but three—it is a perfect infliction to people! And Clotilde, with her strange ideas, will not marry, and so my sweet Marie and Estelle suffer—one does not care to establish the younger before the elder. It is a trial, but it is God's will." Madame Beauvais had become profoundly devout, and, lifting her eyes to Heaven, she would then continue, in a mysterious undertone, "The truth is, Clotilde has a vocation

which we have been slow to recognise,
because we would by no means force it
upon her; but it is evident the child is born
to be a nun. Marriage is contrary to her
character and her tastes. Of course it is a
great trial to us, and we have done our best
to prevent it by giving her every worldly
advantage; but I see it is in vain, and as a
good Christian mother I must be content to
give my child to God—it were sinful to
repine at so high an honour!"

After which tirade Madame Beauvais
would fold her hands in meek complacency,
with an expression which seemed to say,
"Behold a model mother!"

Thus by degrees it became generally
known that Clotilde's vocation was a religious life, and that her repugnance to mar-

riage arose solely from this. She herself
first heard of it abroad, and smiled quietly
at the information, without contradicting it.
From a moderately religious woman, Madame
Beauvais had of late become intensely devotional, attending mass every morning, sitting
patiently through long sermons, never fail-
ing to confess herself at least once a week,
rigidly observing the fasts and festivals,
and last, though not least, entertaining almost daily some priestly guest at her table.
Her younger daughters were not always
either ready or willing to attend her in her
devotional excursions—some little ailment,
some extra fatigue, was a never-failing excuse. So the duty fell to Clotilde, who,
seen thus continually in and out of the
churches, sustained unwittingly the charac-

ter and sentiments which had been imposed upon her. And, in truth, they grew familiar to her. She even persuaded herself they were her own; until at last those quiet hours passed kneeling at the altar became her time of peace and rest, away from the coldness and rebuffs of her father's house. By degrees she withdrew herself more and more from society and her own family; and they, seeing the course events were taking, left her to herself, until attention was once more drawn to her by a renewed proposition of marriage.

The aspirant this time was a man over fifty, a widower, with two young children. He was rich, and his position was good. His first marriage had been of short duration—it was whispered, none of the hap-

piest—and now his family was anxious he
should once more take to himself a wife.
A bachelor's life might prove prejudicial to
his property, and the interests of his children! They urged him to settle himself
again, and busied themselves assiduously in
finding a suitable companion for him. Thus
it was that their eyes fell on Clotilde, who
was just the right age—neither too young
nor too old, of tolerable family, and only
moderate fortune, which balanced nicely
against Monsieur Aubert's fifty years, two
children, name, and wealth. So they proposed to the young lady's parents, who,
beyond measure charmed, accepted eagerly,
but at the same time conditionally. They
were forced to do so, they assured Monsieur
Aubert. "Their sweet Clotilde was of such

an exceptionable character, had such ele-
vated ideas; her soul was far more in heaven than on earth. They could not say
whether she would stoop to listen to worldly proposals, but they gently hinted, if they
failed in persuading her to accept such an
enviable lot, there was her younger sister
Marie, far more suited by taste and inclination to take the direction of Monsieur Aubert's establishment." And so the gentleman bowed smilingly, and assured the
parents that he only desired to be united to
their family—that he knew their daughters
had been so admirably brought up that
they were all equally desirable as wives,
and he left the matter entirely in their
hands. Not as yet knowing the young
ladies personally, he could have no choice;

so, after some consultation, it was agreed
Clotilde should have this one chance more.
At the same time, it was gently insinuated
to her that to be the bride of heaven was
far more likely to bring her happiness than
this earthly marriage—that she had already
trodden so far on the celestial road she
could not well turn back.

"My Clotilde is so susceptible, so sensitive," said Madame Beauvais one afternoon
to her most intimate friend, fully aware
that Clotilde was within earshot, "that
even a union with such a man as Monsieur
Aubert would not ensure her happiness. A
hasty word, a careless look, might pain her,
and I shudder to think what my mother's
heart would suffer to see my child unhappy.
She is not made for the world; only at the

foot of the altar, in the Blessed Virgin's arms, shall I feel assured that her tender heart will be safe from mortal wounds."

Gently the same course of action was insinuated to priest and confessor.

"Guide her to her own happiness, good father; I shall know how to submit," said the saintly mother. "I leave my child in your hands—surely it will be a blessed thing to know she is the sacred bride of heaven!"

And so at home and abroad Clotilde heard the same tale; no voice was raised to bid her stay amongst them. She was just one too many in her home, as she had ever been; no one understood her—no one cared to do so. If she married this Monsieur Aubert, she felt she would be depriving her sister of a husband ; there would still be a striving, a struggling, and, after all, would it bring her any personal satisfaction ?

So matters stood when Clotilde drove out to Lutz to take Jeanne home with her. They had not met for several months. Madame Beauvais had discouraged the intimacy. Jeanne's English ideas were not good for Clotilde, and she feared her influence. A warm friendship, tender sympathy, might only serve to bind Clotilde to the world, and without any too apparent interference, she managed to keep them apart, and Jeanne's busy life had prevented her seeking Clotilde out.

Great, then, was their pleasure on the present occasion. Not that Mademoiselle

Marie permitted them to enjoy each other's society. She kept religiously beside them, fearful lest Jeanne should in any way influence her sister to the injury of her (Marie's) prospects, for looming brightly in the distance was the glory of matrimony. It was well worth fighting for, and so she held her ground manfully, and no word of confidence could the two exchange until late at night, when, the whole household having retired, Clotilde noiselessly found her way to Jeanne's room, and soon the two were seated hand in hand, pouring into each other's ears the anxieties, the sorrows of their young lives.

"Yes," said Clotilde, "I have decided to see this Monsieur Aubert. Not that I dream one moment of marrying him, but just for the form of the thing. Marie will marry him, and be content. Then there will be only Estelle at home, and mamma will be quite happy, and I shall be still and quiet in the convent. I shall have done my duty— no one wants me here!"

" And in the convent, Clotilde, who needs you ? It does not seem to me there is much for you to do there."

" My confessor says the Blessed Mother has ever need of virgins to swell her train ; that in her arms I shall find rest and shelter ; heavenly love to satisfy the utmost craving of my soul. No fear of disappointment there. My life will be complete in itself."

Clotilde paused, a flush of excitement dyeing her cheek, and lighting up her eyes with strange lustre.

" Clotilde, dear," said Jeanne, gently,

"why, then, did God place you in the world?"

But Clotilde did not answer her immediately. She seemed wrapped in her own vision.

"There I need fear nothing. Sinlessly I may pour out my whole soul in love at the foot of the cross. I shall meet with no rebuff—I may lie there in peaceful adoration. If I suffer, it will be in the flesh, and that, by spiritual exercises and penance, I may bring under submission. For why are we thus troubled and anxious? Is it not because of our evil desires? The holy father says my carnal lusts."

"Oh! Clotilde! Clotilde!" almost cried out Jeanne, "what are you saying? What do either you or I know of such things?"

"I know what I feel, and what is explained to me," answered Clotilde, coldly. " Why cannot I be content to marry, like other girls, the first man who asks me? Because,"—and as she spoke she sprang from her seat, and began walking nervously up and down the room—" because I must both love and be loved by my husband; if not, I should be faithless to my vows. I should seek elsewhere that which I did not find in him. My passions roused, I could not stay them with the cold form of duty. Oh! Jeanne, listen to me, dear, for the first and last time. I have never opened my lips to speak before, but I must now; my heart is overflowing."

And throwing herself down beside her friend, she wound her arms about her waist, and thus holding her, spoke quickly.

"Jeanne, I could have loved so easily, and been a good wife and tender mother. I have dreamt sometimes—too often, perhaps, for my own happiness—of the joy of being *two*, yet *one* drawn closer still together by tiny baby hands caressing each in turn— his and mine—that mighty link, that Trinity of love. Thus I would have given myself, freely, gladly; but just as faithful, just as true and loving as I could have been, so should I be equally faithless, equally untrue, wedded to a man I did not love. Look at Louise de la Croix. My heart aches at the very sound of her name; and yet she has no reason to complain. She has won what she played for—a title, wealth, and to be

the acknowledged head of society. With
these objects in view, she married, and what
has been the result?—misery, intense, complete, her name bandied from mouth to mouth,
with little or no respect either for herself
or others. A few days ago she came to see
me, Jeanne. We were a few minutes alone,
and what do you think she did? She took
both my hands in hers, and said, ' Clotilde,
a rumour has reached me that Mr. Aubert
has proposed to you. I know not how you
feel, but for the sake of our early friendship, I would give you one word of warning. Go rather into the convent, Clotilde,
and hush your heart to sleep with *Te Deums*
and Vesper songs, than marry a man you
do not love. Shall I tell you what ought
to be inscribed over the door of almost

every wedding chamber in this our land of
France :—

" He who enters here, leaves hope behind."

Look at me—I have had all I asked for
when a girl, save the one thing I knew not
of, and now I am a miserable woman. If
you cannot marry the man you love, or
remain peaceably in your own home, shelter
yourself within the convent walls. Better
kill your heart than let it slowly bleed to
death. Oh! these *mariages de convenance!*
—they are the very devil's invention for
winning souls to himself, I think!' And
I think so too," continued Clotilde, winding
up with a sort of weary decision. "My
parents are not willing I should remain at
home unmarried; and I will not sell myself, so the convent shall be my refuge. To-

morrow will be my last appearance in the world."

"Oh! Clotilde, dear," said Jeanne, gently stroking the hand she held, while tears filled her eyes, "I could not do it—no, I could not! I love God too, and I love my Saviour, but I have my mother and my friends, all gifts from Him; and then this beautiful fair world! I could not raise a blank wall between it and me, only to catch faint glimpses from time to time of the blue ether overhead. I should be dreaming ever of that wide expanse of sky and sea, so grand, so infinite, making comprehensive to us the mighty, everlasting love. It seems to me as if within that narrow circle my free action, my love would grow narrow too; my heart would not, could not rise

with the same bounding joy, the same glad
aspirations. Like a caged lark, I should
flutter upwards, striving to sing the song of
triumph I had learnt in the free atmosphere of nature ; but the bars of my cage
would beat me down again, and my heart
would break with its overflowing, yet muttered song."

" Ah ! Jeanne, it is well for you to talk
thus ; you love and are beloved, but I have
nothing." Silence fell on the two girls for
a few minutes ; then Clotilde resumed
timidly — " Jeanne, may I ask you one
question ? I would not do so if we were
not so soon to part."

" Ask what you will," said Jeanne, still
full of her last thought.

" Tell me, then, Jeanne—are you at last

going to marry the Count de Lutz?"

White as driven snow grew Jeanne's face, and for a moment she did not answer; at last she said slowly,

" Who told you so, Clotilde ?"

" It is the common talk of all the world. You are always together; he never goes into society. Surely, Jeanne, it is true ?"

" My cousin has never asked me to be his wife since he last returned from Italy. I am with him as I have ever been. I know the estate so well, I am so intimate with his people, we are of necessity thrown much together. There is nothing more, Clotilde."

" Oh! Jeanne, Jeanne, strange rumours are abroad. People say he went to Italy because you would not be his wife. Why did you say him nay? He was so good and noble then!"

" I would not be his wife because I knew he did not love me, Clotilde," said Jeanne sadly.

" And now?" asked her friend.

" Now I wait," said Jeanne, smiling.

" You are playing a hazardous game, Jeanne. Men do not often ask a woman three times."

" I know it," said Jeanne. " But, Clotilde dear, I would rather not talk of this ;" and rising from her seat, she moved towards the mantelpiece, and stood leaning against it.

Clotilde followed her, and laid her hand upon her, saying,

" Jeanne, at the risk of displeasing you, I

must speak. We are neither of us children now, but women. For me the battle of the world is over, but you are in the midst of it, and, unless I am much mistaken, it will rage strong and fierce around you. I have loved you well, Jeanne—better than any of my companions—better than my own sisters; you are my only regret; and now I must give you just one word of warning. It is all I can do—the whole world seems determined to blind you. You do not know your friends from your enemies—you do not see where you are treading."

"Have I any enemies?" said Jeanne, opening her eyes in sheer astonishment.

"I am afraid so," said Clotilde.

"Where and who are they?" asked Jeanne.

"You know her well, Jeanne, and will meet her at the ball to-morrow night. I was speaking of her just now—La Marquise de la Croix."

"Oh! Clotilde, she and I have nothing in common. I do not think she can harm me much."

"Alas! far more than you dream of, Jeanne, I fear," replied Clotilde, seriously. "Listen to me, for you shall know how matters stand. For years the Marquise has loved the Count de Lutz—it dates as far back as the last ball given at the Château. After that she sought him out in Paris, and forced her intimacy upon him. What they were to each other, the world can never know. All of a sudden the Count left Paris, and went to Rome; she followed

him ; he disappeared, and few people doubt,
notwithstanding her persistent denial, that
she knew his whereabouts. She has been
backwards and forwards in Italy for the
last three years. Since the Count's return,
she has tried in vain to see him ; you know
how he shuts himself up, and has refused to
see anyone. It has exasperated Louise, and
driven her to say many things which, in her
right mind, she would never have said. She
speaks of him as a martyr, and your mother
as an *intrigante,* who still holds him bound
to you by the promise he made your father ;
and of you she speaks as of the worst co-
quette—you will not be his wife, because
Gordon Elliot is your real lover ; that you
play one against the other, and hold them
both in chains. She hints at even worse

things, Jeanne, but I cannot bring my lips to utter them."

Wider and wider Jeanne opened her eyes as she listened in silence. At last she said,

"Clotilde, how dare she talk thus! Does she take my cousin for an idiot?"

"No, but she is in love, Jeanne, and hardly takes the trouble to hide it. Her husband is rarely or ever with her. She has been staying at Amonville with her mother for the last six months, ostensibly for her health; but all the world knows it is to be near the Count, and she has not yet seen him. It is dangerous thus to thwart such a woman."

"She must be either mad or very wicked," said Jeanne, seriously. "What does she do it for? She cannot marry my cousin."

"Oh! Jeanne, how innocent you are!" said Clotilde, half laughing. "Do you not understand she would have the Count for her lover—her very humble servant and adorer? Why, Jeanne, there is hardly a woman in Paris who has not some such *liaison*. It is hateful to think of, but it is nevertheless true. They do not know what love means before marriage, and they pay dearly for it afterwards. Do you understand now why, knowing myself as I do— knowing the temptations to which I should be exposed, the society into which I should be thrown—I choose a convent life?"

"Yes," said Jeanne—"I understand, Clotilde; but I never till to-day heard of my cousin's intimacy with the Marquise—

things of that sort are rarely spoken of at
the Cottage. I know that great and crying
evils exist, but in my country home I do
not realize them as facts. Moreover, I
know nothing of Charles's life for the last
two years. When he came home, he desired no questions might be asked, and as
he is a free man, living on his own lands,
in his own château, answerable to no man
for his actions, we could not but respect his
request, even had we felt inclined to do
otherwise. That he may have committed
errors—sins, even—is quite possible—who
amongst us is perfect?—but that he has
acted dishonourably, let it be by whom it
may, that I do not believe, and never shall,
until he tells me so himself. I will hear
nothing more on that subject; it is no busi-

ness of mine. Louise herself is deeply to
be pitied."

Jeanne's usually pale face had flushed
deeply while she spoke, and her eyes were
dark with emotion.

"Ah! well; forgive me, Jeanne, if I
have vexed you," said Clotilde. "I would
only have warned you. We have all of us
an evil genius in our lives, and I have a presentiment that Madame de la Croix will be
yours!"

"She cannot harm me if I am guilty of no
wrong," said Jeanne, proudly.

"Ah! Jeanne, dear, our foot slips sometimes before we know it ourselves. What
woman amongst us has not her weak
point?"

"True," answered Jeanne, meekly bowing her head ; the arrow had struck home.

" And now, Jeanne, good night, and God bless you, dear! Soon there will be nothing left for me to do but to pray that the dangers and temptations of this world may be kept from you."

" Nay, rather pray, Clotilde, that I may be kept 'unspotted from the world.' I do not shrink from the fight, I do not wish to be exempt from it, but I do pray, I do hope to come forth purified from the fire. Good night, dear."

Tenderly they embraced, and without another word, but with full hearts and tearful eyes they parted. Once alone, Jeanne sat thinking, thinking deeply, as we do when light is suddenly thrown upon what has hitherto seemed a mystery to us. She never for one moment imagined her cousin had been guilty of any wrong towards the Marquise; a mistake, an error, doubtless. Yes. Under what form or shape she did not pause to examine. All his past conduct was clear to her; his dislike to society, his long absence, his deep depression. The Count was not the man to do a wrong, and not repent it; at least, so Jeanne judged him, and though she grieved, she did not love the sinner less.

After a time she undressed herself slowly, thinking all the while; and, kneeling down beside her bed, prayed earnestly, prayed for forgiveness for herself and others, even for her enemies. Then she laid herself to rest, a smile upon her lips, and peace, the peace of innocence, on brow and heart.

CHAPTER IX.

THE following evening, as in years gone by, Clotilde Beauvais and Jeanne de Lutz entered the ball-room arm-in-arm. Both were dressed alike, in spotless white. It had been Clotilde's earnest desire, and Jeanne had willingly agreed. Long flowing robes of airy texture, lilies of the valley in their hair and on their bosoms, strings of fine pearls about their necks—thus were they adorned. And just as pure and chaste as in her early girlhood Jeanne looked that night; only there was something more,

namely, the full, perfected beauty of the
woman. The *contour* of her face and figure
was as delicate as ever, but there was a
roundness, a completeness now, only to be
met with in early womanhood. Her expression had grown too; her grey eyes were
fuller and deeper; you could look into their
depths as into a clear mountain stream; her
lips were richly curved, sweet, and restful.
The quiet happiness of the last few months
shone out in her whole being. Thus Jeanne
had ripened outwardly into perfect womanhood.

The friends formed a strange contrast,
the one so winning and graceful, the other
so stern and cold; and yet Clotilde had perhaps never looked so well as she did this
night. Her dress was becoming to her, and

then she was glad to be with, and proud of,
Jeanne.   It was her last worldly feeling;
and as she moved through the crowd, with
her head erect and her distant manner, she
seemed to express the feeling in reality uppermost in her heart.

"I am with you for the last time; but
even now I have ceased to be of you."

Their entrance thus together created somewhat of a sensation.   Jeanne de Lutz so
seldom showed herself in public; and it was
generally whispered that the ball was given
in honour of the rich Monsieur Aubert, who
had proposed for one of the three sisters—it
was believed Clotilde.   But of all those
who lifted their heads and fixed their eyes
on Jeanne as she entered the salon, none
did so with such feverish haste as the

Marquise de la Croix. It was no kindly glance she cast upon her former companion, but one of eager, anxious scrutiny.

"I see nothing in her—she is no beauty at all," was her involuntary exclamation as she followed Jeanne's every movement.

"Whom are you speaking of?" asked her neighbour, a lady many years older than herself, and who had known the Marquise from early childhood.

"Jeanne de Lutz, of course," was the impatient answer. "Just look at her!— what affectation to appear all in white, as if she were already a bride! It does not suit her—she is far too pale—she looks like a ghost; her eyes are too large for her face; and her hair is decidedly English. I never thought it was so red!"

A smile, which she tried in vain to repress, overspread her companion's face. She was a kindly woman, and pitied the jealous anger of her younger sister, for she knew only too well the source from whence it sprang, and she ventured to say,

" Hush! Louise, or people will be accusing you of jealousy. Jeanne de Lutz may not be actually beautiful, but she has a marvellous charm and grace about her. Do not array yourself against her—it will be a losing game for you, I fear. Go your way, and let her go hers. You are the most beautiful woman of the two; but you have this yet to learn—that there is a something far more powerful than mere beauty of form or face—a something, I cannot give it a name, wholly independent of personal charms, and which exercises a deeper and more lasting influence on men. If I am not mistaken, Jeanne de Lutz possesses that gift in no ordinary degree."

" I neither know nor care what she is possessed of," answered Louise, in a low, passionate voice; and, rising from her seat, she moved away, her haughty face express· ive of more than one evil passion.

Yet there was a strange attractive beauty about her. Her great black eyes were wild with unsatisfied desire ; her richly-developed frame was well calculated to attract the attention of the most casual observer. Beside her Jeanne looked a mere shadow, a child floating through the dance, both giving and receiving pleasure. At first the thought that this night was to seal Clotilde's fate, that it was the last time she would be amongst them, made the music and the gaiety jar upon Jeanne's senses ; but gradually, when she saw how Clotilde herself cast all care for the future away, how she talked and smiled, and allowed Monsieur Aubert to approach her, listening with grave propriety to his somewhat fulsome compliments, it seemed to her as if the conversation of the previous evening were but an evil dream ; and as such she tried to forget it, and join heartily in the present enjoyment.

Once only, towards the end of the evening, Clotilde's words came back to her— "We have all our evil genius, Jeanne, and I have a presentiment Louise de la Croix is yours."

It happened thus : Jeanne was resting after a dance, when she heard a voice close to her say, " Mademoiselle de Lutz forgets her friends easily." She knew at once who it was that spoke, and with difficulty kept down the rising colour.

" Pardon me, Louise," she said calmly, holding out her hand. " I have tried several times to speak to you this evening, but have never been able to reach you at an opportune moment."

" I can understand that," answered Louise. " I think you are alone here. It is certain-ly difficult for a young girl to move freely about a ball-room when she has no chaperon to keep her in countenance."

Jeanne understood the innuendo, and it was on her lips to answer, " I am Madame

Beauvais' guest," but she checked herself—
it was not worth while—and merely observed carelessly that "the rooms were very
crowded and somewhat hot."

"Yes," said Louise, "they are very hot.
Supposing we go into the conservatory a
little—I have something to say to you—will
you come, Jeanne?"

It would have been difficult to refuse,
and so, excusing herself to her partner,
Jeanne took the Marquise's proffered arm,
and, thus linked together, they threaded
their way through the crowded saloons.
On their passage, they passed close by Clotilde.   Jeanne's eyes met hers, and a cold
shiver ran through her frame as she inter-
preted her friend's look of anxious, tender surprise.   But the Marquise drew her

on, until they reached the conservatory.

" It is cooler here," said that lady, seating herself in a remote corner, where the green shrubs and flowers effectually hid her from public view, and drawing another low chair to her side. " Come and rest, Jeanne," she said ; " ball-rooms are always fatiguing places, even when one is accustomed to them ; but to you, who so seldom frequent them, they must be doubly so."

" I am not in the least tired," said Jeanne, as she took the proffered seat.

" I am, then," said Louise ; " the heat and crowd tire me. The Beauvais never do manage things properly. If they must invite such a medley, they should have given two balls instead of one, crowding the rooms to suffocation, and throwing to-

gether people who are not accustomed to
meet each other."

"All are free to come or not, as they
choose. I do not see that anyone has a
right to complain ; they could have stayed
away."

"Most wisely said, Mademoiselle Jeanne,"
rejoined the Marquise, with a mock bow ;
"and I should most certainly have followed
your advice, except for a private reason of
my own. Others may have done the same.
Can you guess what my reason for coming
here to-night was ?"

Jeanne contented herself with shaking
her head ; the tone of the conversation dis-
pleased her.

"Well, then, I will tell you," continued
the Marquise. "I came to meet you."

"I am highly honoured," answered Jeanne coldly, never lifting her eyes from the ground.

"Nay," replied the Marquise, "you are but a pretext—a means to an end."

Jeanne was perfectly silent, though at each word the Marquise uttered her colour went and came.

"Mademoiselle de Lutz, will you render me a service?" asked the Marquise, with sudden abruptness.

"It depends on what the service is," was the quiet answer.

Up rose the Marquise from her seat, her face flushed, her whole frame quivering with emotion. A fierce struggle was going on within her. Should she stoop to ask a favour—to confess her weakness to her rival?—for that Jeanne was her rival she never for one moment doubted. At that moment jealousy, love, hate, were warring within her for the mastery, and love conquered.

"Jeanne," she said, going up to her, and speaking in low, softened tones—"Jeanne, I must see your cousin—I must see the Count de Lutz."

"The way to the Château is open," answered Jeanne, coldly.

"And the door closed," replied the Marquise, quickly. A dead silence fell upon them both. "Jeanne, you will procure me an interview?" said Louise, at last.

"I have nothing to do with my cousin's movements. I am not mistress of the Château," was the answer.

" If rumour speaks rightly, you either are or ought to be," answered Louise.

" I know nothing about rumours—they never reach me," replied Jeanne.

" Better, perhaps, if they did," answered Louise. Checking herself quickly, she tried to take Jeanne's hand, but the young girl drew back. " Jeanne, it were wiser for us to be friends than enemies," exclaimed the Marquise.

" I am neither one nor the other," answered Jeanne.

" Then in pity help me," murmured Louise. " Let me see the Count for ten minutes—I ask but that!"

" And I reply," answered Jeanne, for the first time lifting her head, and drawing herself up to her full height, " that I have neither the will nor the power to grant your request. If the Count de Lutz chooses to close his gates against all the world, or to open them and welcome the whole of Europe, it is no business of mine. I have nothing to do in the matter. But, once for all, Madame la Marquise, understand I will not be mixed up in your intrigues. How dare you, a wedded wife, thus demean yourself? "

As the last words fell full and clear from Jeanne's lips, a mocking laugh rang through the conservatory, so sharp and ringing that it attracted the attention of some stragglers like themselves, who turned and looked at the two ladies.

" Really, Mademoiselle de Lutz, you are too witty to-night!" exclaimed the Marquise,

checking her laughter. "It is astonishing
with what facility you appreciate a joke. I
am no longer astonished that the Count finds
his retreat at Lutz so charming. Pray present my compliments to him, and if ever I
can render you a service, you will find me
your humble servant. I think I will return
to the salon. Good evening." And gathering her cloak about her, she passed out of
the conservatory,

Left thus alone, Jeanne grew quite still.
A great trouble seemed to overshadow her.
Had she been too hasty? Had she made a
mistake? Oh! what was this mystery
which seemed gradually enclosing her?

"What is it—what can it be?" she murmured to herself. Alas! she was beating
against a rock! Be still, Jeanne, be still!

Light will come only too soon ! Be thankful for the present darkness !

Worn out and weary, Jeanne sought her bed, almost as morning dawned, and fell at once into a deep, heavy slumber. Was it an over-vivid dream, or was it reality that roused her ? It seemed as though some one were stooping over her, tenderly, lingeringly kissing her on cheek and brow. She opened her eyes and sat up, only in time to hear her room door close softly, and to feel warm tears still wet upon her face. All was still and silent around, but on the table beside her bed her eye fell on a folded note. Opening it hurriedly, she read as follows:—

" Good-bye, dear, gentle Jeanne, my one regret in bidding farewell to the world!

I am going where I shall pray for you
night and day; for, oh! I am very fearful
for you! Remember, dearest, my last words
—my great presentiment. Beware of Louise
de la Croix! I know, I feel sure she will
work you ill. Farewell for the last time,
Jeannette.

"Your old friend,

"CLOTILDE BEAUVAIS.

"From henceforth 'Sister Agatha.'"

Scarcely had she seized the sense of the
letter, when, springing from her bed, and
throwing a wrapper around her, she ran
towards Clotilde's room. At the same moment the roll of carriage wheels attracted
her attention. Hardly knowing what she
did, she threw open the staircase window,

and looked out on the courtyard below. She
was just in time to see the Beauvais's private
coupé pass out under the *porte-cochère*. Then
she knew it was too late.

" Oh ! Clotilde ! Clotilde !" she exclaimed.

A door opposite opened, and Madame
Beauvais made her appearance.

" Vous désirez quelque chose, Jeanne?"
she asked politely.

Jeanne, unable to speak, pointed in silence
in the direction the carriage had taken.

" Ah, yes," said Madame, " Clotilde decided herself last night, and desired that the
carriage might come round early this morning. She particularly did not wish to dis-
turb you. Of course it is a heavy trial for
me ; but ' God's will be done !' " And
therewith she heaved a profound sigh, crossed

herself, cast her eyes up to the ceiling, and then, recovering herself, continued, " After all, I feel she has done wisely—she was not fit for the world ; and though too much of a gentleman to say so, Monsieur Aubert decidedly shows a preference for Marie. Think, my dear Jeanne, what a comfort it will be to feel one daughter the bride of Heaven, and another the wife of such a man. But had you not better return to your room?—you will catch cold standing at this open window. It is still very early. I will send my maid to you with a cup of chocolate. But take my advice, and rest a little longer."

Silently Jeanne obeyed, and re-entered her room, but not to rest. Bitter were the tears she shed over her lost friend in her living tomb. Once only again in life did Jeanne de Lutz and Clotilde Beauvais meet. Let it be recorded here, though it was many years later, when sorrow and the world had left deep traces on Jeanne's face and heart. One Eastertide, or, rather, one Holy Thursday, she had driven into Amonville, alone, on business, and, leaving the carriage in the High Street, had wended her way into some of the old and less frequented parts of the town. Suddenly she found herself in a narrow, unpaved street, with high walls rising on either side, from within which strains of the richest music came forth, breaking the stillness. Jeanne paused and listened. A woman, dressed in her best, carrying a little child, passed her.

" What convent is this?" asked Jeanne.

" Le Couvent de l'Adoration Perpétuelle,
Madame," answered the woman ; adding,
" The entrance is up yonder. That little
door you see in the wall."

" Thank you," answered Jeanne ; and
she followed her informer, who herself disappeared by the door she had indicated.

Several women, carrying infants in their
arms, or holding children by the hand,
passed her on their way to or from the
chapel. She knew well what it meant—the
pious pilgrimage of the seven churches.
Penetrating the narrow passage, she entered
the chapel. There light and harmony greeted
her. The chapel was little larger than a
room—a gallery ran round the upper part,
where shadowy, ghost-like forms knelt motionless. The altar itself was one blaze of

light; one gorgeous display of flowers, rising out of the midst of which was the veiled crucifix. In front of the altar, on a velvet cushion, lay a small silver crucifix, before which all those who entered knelt reverently, and kissed the five wounds of the Christ. Children in their mothers' arms stooped down, and with their rosy lips pressed the cold silver. On either side of the altar two figures, bent almost to the ground, kept watch. Their robes and veils were white, but hanging from their shoulders were long scarlet cloaks, without seam, woven from the top throughout—typical of that scarlet vestment for which the impious cast lots.

Jeanne glided to an empty chair close by the altar, underneath the gallery, and opposite a little door leading into the convent, and used by the nuns for going in and out of the chapel. She was very weary that day—not in body only, but in heart and mind. Life seemed so long; and yet she did not dare to wish to die! So with folded hands she knelt gazing on the veiled Christ, half wondering if in truth his face was hidden from her for ever. Her whole attitude was one of prayer, and yet she was not praying, only resting in a sort of trance-like stupor. The song of the nuns seemed to reach her from afar; the faint smell of the incense seemed to lull her senses, so she knelt on. Suddenly a slight movement, a gliding of figures to and fro, roused her. She looked up; the nuns at the altar had risen, and were slowly bowing low, even to the ground, before retiring. Their watch was over.

At the same moment the door near Jeanne opened, and two figures, robed like the other two in white, with the same scarlet cloaks, issued slowly forth. Mechanically Jeanne followed them with her eyes. Suddenly her whole face changed to one of eager gladness, for beneath the white coif, in the stern, colourless face and downcast eyes of the foremost nun, she recognised the friend of her girlhood, her whom she had so grieved after. As the nun was sweeping past her, Jeanne, without thinking, with wild impulse, stretched forth her hand, while from between her closed lips the words escaped—

"Oh! Clotilde, dear, pray for me!"

The voice, the name, both so long unheard, stayed the nun's steps. She looked
down on Jeanne's upturned face, as we
might look at some dead friend arisen suddenly from the grave, changed, yet familiar
to us. Was this sad woman, with the tearful eyes, entreating to be prayed for, the
same as the fair girl, all robed in white,
whom she had last seen in a ball-room?

"Sister Agatha!" said the nun behind,
sternly, and thus recalled to time and
place, "Sister Agatha," or Clotilde Beauvais,
moved on; but even as she did so, Jeanne
thought she caught the muttered syllables,
" I do, I do!" and bowing her head upon
her *prie-dieu*, she, too, wept and prayed.
But when Jeanne rose at last, and left the
chapel, she was comforted. Looking back

on the threshold, her gaze rested for the last time on the kneeling figure of her friend, and a sort of gladness came over her; at least, she left one praying for her.

Early the morning after the ball Madame de Lutz drove over to fetch her daughter. During the homeward drive Jeanne told her mother all that had taken place, always excepting the episode relative to Madame de la Croix and the Count. That was sacred, buried in her own heart.

After listening attentively to her tale, Madame said,

" We also have news for *you*, Jeanne !"

" What news ?" she asked, carelessly, thinking only of some little household change.

"I had a letter from Gordon yesterday," continued Madame, "in which he tells me his father is dangerously ill, that he has had a stroke of paralysis, and that there is no hope of his ultimate recovery. And my brother is now most anxious, feverishly anxious, Gordon writes, to see both myself and you, Jeanne. He and I are the last of a large family of brothers and sisters, and it is ten years since we met; so I have decided to go without further delay. Everything is arranged for us to leave Amonville by tonight's train, and I have written for Gordon to meet us at Southampton the day after tomorrow."

"You nearly take away my breath, mamma," answered Jeanne, trying to hide her emotion; for, as a bird flies back to its nest, so her thoughts had flown home to her beloved.

" Miss Ivor and I have decided, Jeanne, that, after the first week or two, it would be as well for you not to remain at your uncle's; you barely know each other, and he will scarcely miss you, so we have agreed together that you shall go with Miss Ivor to Brighton.   Her sister, Mrs. Norton, is there at present, and the entire change and sea-air will do you good.   I think you need a little of both.   You have had quite nursing and worry enough for the last twelv emonths. I do not care for you to go through the same ordeal again."

" But, mamma, I do not know Mrs. Norton," said Jeanne.   " Will she not view me somewhat in the light of an intruder?   It is not often Amie goes among her own people, and a stranger is always more or less in the way."

"Nay, nay, Jeanne," responded Miss Ivor, "there are exceptions to every rule. My sister knows you so well by hearsay that you can scarcely call yourself a stranger; and she knows, moreover, all that you and your mother have been to me. She will only be too glad to pay a tithe of the debt, if that be possible."

"Thank you, Amie," said Jeanne, bending forward, and holding up her face to kiss her friend. Then Miss Ivor saw that her eyes were full of suppressed tears. A link in Jeanne's chain had been snapped away that morning, and now a finer and more precious one seemed gradually loosening itself.

The remainder of the day was spent in the bustle of departure. There was little time left for thought, less still for regret. It was almost evening before she saw her cousin. She was busily engaged in the boudoir, stowing away her own especial treasures, when he entered.

"So you have come home only to be off again," he remarked, after the first greeting, and throwing himself wearily into one of the few unencumbered arm-chairs.

"Yes," said Jeanne quietly; and looking at him, she noticed the wan, anxious expression of his face, so added—"You will take care of yourself, Charles, while we are away, and not over-work yourself?"

" I will do my best," he answered, carelessly ; " but I shall be very left-handed,
Jeanne."

She made no reply, but stooped busily
over her open trunk. At last, as if to
change the conversation, she said,

" Charles, Madame de la Croix was at
the ball last night."

" I suppose so," he answered.

" She desires to see you—desires it most
earnestly," continued Jeanne, without raising
her head.

" Did she commission you to tell me so ?"
asked the Count, rising, and approaching
Jeanne.

" She begged—she entreated me to procure her an interview with you," answered
Jeanne ; " and I told her I had nothing to

do with your movements—that you were
your own master, and that, if you closed
your château gates against your friends, you
did so advisedly ; and so we parted not the
best of friends ?"

" Is that all she said ?" asked the Count,
sternly.

" All I care to tell you," answered Jeanne,
moving away.

There was a dead silence ; then the
Count, following her, laid his hand upon
her shoulder, and said, with suppressed
emotion, " I will not ask you what she said,
Jeanne, or what you have heard in Amonville concerning her and me. I guess pretty
well the sum-total of the whole. But this
I will tell you, and I think you will not
doubt my word—Madame de la Croix has

never been anything to me but the most ordinary acquaintance. I have never shown her more than the usual civilities due from a gentleman to a lady. I have never sought her society, or thrown myself in her way, and it is now full two years since I last saw her."

"And in Italy?" asked Jeanne, eagerly lifting her head, and looking at him. So flashing was that look, so deep and full that gaze, that a glimmering of light shot to the Count's heart. One moment of agonizing, startling pain, then he cast it from him. No, no, it could not, must not be—he would not see! He might suffer, but not she—not his gentle Jeanne; so, steadying himself once more, he answered calmly,

"After the first year I never saw her, Jeanne. I was not in Rome; and she knew my whereabout no better than you did yourself."

Restlessly Jeanne moved about the room —restlessly—like one in pain. With anxious gaze the Count followed her every movement. His handsome face grew dark, his lips compressed; he had felt the awakening touch, and love and passion were now fighting for the mastery. A couple of strides took him once more to her side, then he spoke again—low, so low that, had the room been full, his words could have reached no ear but hers.

"Jeanne, remember you would not be my wife under the linden trees." Then he took her head between his two hands, looked steadfastly into the pale speaking face, and closing her answering lips with one long kiss, turned, and left the room. Across the garden walk he went, through the meadows, full of butter-cups and daisies, beneath the forest trees just budding forth in their first Spring-tide beauty, in the growing stillness of coming night he hastened on, and never paused until he had crossed his own threshold. Entering the studio, he threw himself with a smothered cry into an arm-chair, and burying his face in his hands, wept, as men weep but once in their lives. Yes, he loved her now, and he knew it too!

And Jeanne?—she stood still where he had left her, that kiss upon her lips filling her whole soul. She was satisfied, she was glad—at last he loved her. A thousand little things came thronging back to her memory—how blind she had been!—how blind! Others had seen it—all the world save herself. Hence doubtless all those rumours Clotilde had told her of, and which had so troubled her. She smiled softly, gladly to herself, repeating, half aloud, his last words—

"Jeanne, remember you would not be my wife under the linden trees."

So that was it—the pride of the De Lutzes. Once, twice, he had sought her hand—he would not plead again ; she must go to him, so would he be revenged. And Jeanne laughed, laughed to herself as she walked up and down the room. And yet there was a secret feeling, a sort of struggle within her, warring against her love. How could she go to him and tell him she was ready now to be his wife? What would he say?—what would he think of her? And yet he loved her! Thrilling through her heart for the first time came that great certainty.

In this crisis of our mutual lives a man may be mistaken, but a woman never is— her instinct serves her.

Then there rushed on Jeanne the remembrance that a few hours, and they would be parted—land and sea between them. Why had he left her thus abruptly? Should she not see him again? A sort of terror seized her; all the partings of former days, the death-agony she had so lately struggled through, came back to her. No, she could not bear it again, she could not, when a word from her, only one little word perhaps, was needed to heal the gaping wound of pride, and make him all her own. Jeanne did not *think* now, she only *felt* thought and reason were alike losing their hold over her—love was in the ascendancy. Catching up a shawl from the sofa, she threw it round her, ran quickly from her own room to the drawing-room, and, throwing open the window, stepped out upon the balcony, straining her eyes in the direction of the Château; but Charles de Lütz had long since disappeared.

A moment's hesitation; then Jeanne ran down the steps, along the garden path he had trod only a few minutes before, and, in her turn, never paused until she stood at the door of the studio, with her hand upon the lock. Only for one moment did she hesitate; then she opened the door, and entered with quick steps the room she had left so carelessly only three days before. The Spring day was fast drawing to a close, twilight was creeping on. In front of the empty hearth, his hands resting on the marble mantelpiece, his head bent, and his face sad and stern, stood Charles de Lutz. Straight up to him Jeanne went, and laid her hand upon his shoulder. He did not start, he did not turn, he felt whose hand it was, and his whole frame responded to the touch.

"Jeanne," he said, "I thought you were at home."

"So I was," she answered; "but I have

come here once more. Charles, I am going away."

Now he turned and looked at her, her face was very pale, and her eyes, as she raised them to his, were pleadingly, agonizingly sad. She was frightened—he was so cold; a chill was creeping over her heart.

"Jeanne, child, it is too late for you to be out. The night is cold—go home, dear."

His voice sounded forced and hollow. Jeanne tried to speak, she tried to answer him, but her white lips were silent, the words would not come. Did he not see? Could he not forgive her?

"Jeanne, Jeanne, go!" said the Count, almost fiercely; but even as he spoke he took her hands in both of his, crushing them in his powerful grasp, till Jeanne moaned out in pain.

"What brought you here, Jeannette— what brought you?" said the Count. "Leave me alone, child, to my solitude. You can-not, must not love me!"

"But I do, I do!" cried Jeanne. "Oh! Charles, forgive me!"

She stood close beside him now, her sweet womanly face raised to his, and the rich blood mantling cheek and brow. What could he do, that man with the full heart and loving nature? What could he do, save gather her to his bosom, and cover hands, face, hair with kisses? A delirium of joy overwhelmed Jeanne, bathing her soul in the clear sparkling waters of a deep,

true love. Closer she nestled in his arms,
lying there at rest at last, the struggle, and
the fever, and the battle over. No thought
of the past, no dream of the future, interfer-
ing with the present moment. It was complete in itself—perfect! And yet, holding
her thus, Charles de Lutz did not speak, he
did not say,

"Forgive, me darling, I love you too, and
would not lose you, or let you go, for aught
in this world! I was but trying you, to see
the strength of your love, sweet one!"

No, he did not speak, but stood holding
her to him. Jeanne could hear the quick,
loud beating of his heart, but she could not
see his flashing eyes, and his whole form,
erect, defiant, as if in every corner of the
room, out of every shadow, he saw a hand

stretched forth to steal his treasure out of his very arms.

A few minutes of that stillness, and Jeanne raised her drooping head, and passed one arm familiarly, as in her childish days, around his neck, thus drawing his face down almost on a level with her own. The look in his eyes startled her. She remembered he had not spoken to her. What had she done? Had she shocked him with her lack of maidenly reserve? The happiness was marred, the brief joy troubled.

" Charles, speak to me," she murmured. "Tell me that you love me now."

" Be still, my darling—be still for one minute longer," said the Count, pleadingly, and he drew her closer to him, holding her to his heart; he could not let her go. Would she ever come fluttering back again of her own sweet will?

Obedient as a little child in her perfect love and faith, she laid her head once more upon his shoulder and waited.

"Oh! Jeanne! oh! my darling!—too late! too late!" half groaned the Count, while a fierce struggle seemed almost to convulse his features. Gently he stroked her hair back from her forehead, lingeringly, as if he were loth to withdraw his hand.

"Jeannette," he said at last, "I have a tale to tell. Can you listen to me, darling?"

Low and sad was his voice, very white his face; he was evidently under strong self-control, striving to command his words, his actions, his very thoughts.

Jeanne looked up smiling, throwing back her head with soft gladness. " He had a tale to tell." She had known it all along. Of course he had—that old, old tale, still ever new and fresh to each of us in turn, which she had waited for; that strain of music floating round the world, and never losing its first harmony; the last best gift God gave to man to comfort and to strengthen him; the perfume from the sweetest flower He culled and bore with Him out of the sacred garden.

Gently, tenderly, the Count placed Jeanne in his own arm-chair, where he had passed so many hours of weary sickness, with her to minister beside him. Then he once more took her hand, saying, " Let me hold it yet a little longer, Jeanne?"

She turned a troubled look upon him.
Did he not understand her? Had he not
heard she loved him? Why then should he
not take his own?

CHAPTER X.

" JEANNETTE, it is growing dark. Shall
I light the lamp, dear ?"

She nodded her assent; and, rising, he
lifted a small Roman lamp of curicus work-
manship from off a richly-carved oak-bracket
occupying one corner of the room, and in a
few minutes a soft subdued light overpowered
the last rays of day; and then the Count
returned to Jeanne's side, and, kneeling
down beside her, took both her hands in
his, saying, in a voice of deep emotion,

" Jeannette, darling, from the hour of

your birth unto this day I have had but one
thought, one wish as regards yourself—that
of caring for you, of sparing you even the
shadow of pain or sorrow. You were to
have been my wife. I loved you as one
loves something that is one's own, of the
possession of which one has never doubted;
you were pure, and good, and fair, ignorant
of the world. How could I dream that
your woman's heart, expanding of itself,
would learn the difference between a brother's and a lover's love? When you
refused to be my wife, I took it as a childish whim, a lesson learnt from your mother,
and was more angered than really hurt.
That feeling grew later. After all, you
were right, Jeanne, I never really loved you
until a dying man I awoke, beneath my own

ancestral roof, in the dim twilight, and saw
an angel kneeling at my hearth—an angel
I thought you, Jeanne, until I learnt to
recognise in you something more fitted for
the daily food of our poor human hearts—
a perfect woman; and even then I knew
not that I loved you.   I had no right to do
so.   Alas! the human heart will claim its
own, come what may.   I know I love
you now, my darling, with all the best,
the finest instincts of my nature, with the
tenderness of a mother for a child, a man
for the wife of his bosom.   I would fain
take you in my arms, hide you from all the
world, shield and shelter you from   the
slightest blast of evil.   Oh, Jeanne, Jeanne,
do men's hearts ever break with sorrow?
If so, I think mine must.   Never again

may I speak of love to you, dear, never
again may I call you my beloved. Ready
to lay down my life for you, yet knowing
I must wound you to the very quick.
Jeanne, forgive me, dear; and may God
help both you and me to bear our common
lot!"

He bowed his head low upon her lap,
seeking for strength; and she, stooping over
him with her angel face, wound her arms
about him, and sought to comfort him. She
knew now that a great sorrow was over-
shadowing her—that the mystery of his life
would darken hers; but she knew, too, that
no barrier rising between them, no sin he
might have committed, could alter the fact
that she loved him—not with one of those
every-day affections which flourish only

while the sun shines, but with a love which
formed the chief part of her being—which
had borne much, but which knew itself capable of bearing more.

"Tell me what our trouble is, Charles;
we can but share it," said Jeanne gently.

"And be parted, Jeanne."

"Let us hope not quite," she answered.
"Tell me—pray, tell me quickly!" And the
white, anxious face was lifted pleadingly to
him, as he now stood before her.

"You have never asked me the secret of
those three years of absence, darling. You
must solve it now. Look!" As he spoke,
he went to a secretary, unlocked, and drew
forth a packet, which he laid in Jeanne's
lap, saying, "I never thought you would
read it till I was far away or dead; now it

is yours. I have not the courage to tell the tale, Jeanne—pardon me. I am another woman's husband !"

A sharp cry of pain parted the girl's lips, and she rose as if to fly.

" Jeanne, listen to me," said the Count, throwing himself in her way, and speaking passionately. " Remember you cast me off. I have a right to be heard. Wilfully, knowingly, I have not wronged you. I tell you, it is only within the last few days that I have even suspected that I loved you with other than a brother's love. And you—you were so calm, so self-possessed ; how could I guess your heart throbbed for me ? Oh ! Jeanne, I erred in one moment of passion ! My life is wrecked, all hope is dead within me ; but I would gladly suffer ten thousand times more, rather than have brought this misery on you."

Jeanne did not speak. She was wounded —all over wounded—in her love, in her pride, in her woman's dignity. She only shivered visibly.

"Child, child!" exclaimed the Count, looking at her, and the agony of his voice vibrated through her whole frame—"have you no word, cannot you pardon me?" He took her passive hands in his, and covered them with kisses.

She did not shrink from him, no sound of reproach parted her pale lips, but raising her eyes to him like a stricken deer, she murmured,

"Take me home, Charles—take me to my mother."

He awaited no second bidding. Catching up a large travelling-cloak that lay close at hand, he threw it over her; then, taking her in his arms, strode towards the cottage. Fortunately, Miss Ivor met them on the threshold. Before she could speak, the Count had said, in quick, harsh tones,

"I think I have killed her, Miss Ivor."

A presentiment of the truth shot through the Englishwoman's heart, but she had presence of mind enough to throw open the door of her room, and sign to the Count to lay her on her bed. He did so, and then stood gazing down upon the insensible marble-like face, while Miss Ivor chafed her hands and bathed her brow with Eau de Cologne.

"How did it happen?" she asked, feeling

that anything was better than the Count's dead silence. " How did it happen ?" she repeated.

" Why, we have discovered too late that we love each other, as well as even my aunt could desire; only, unfortunately, I am a married man, and cannot make Jeanne my wife now ; and so we must part. Thus much for your English system !" And he laughed a mocking laugh. It seemed to rouse Jeanne. She half opened her eyes.

" Go," said Miss Ivor, turning to the Count peremptorily, her usually quiet face expressive of angry indignation.

One more look of mingled love and pain the Count turned upon Jeanne, and then he obeyed. Once in the hall, he passed his hand across his brow, like a man trying to

drive away an evil vision, then slowly he
directed his steps towards his aunt's room.
He found her still in the midst of her preparations for departure, and her first word
of greeting was,

"Where is Jeanne?"

"With Miss Ivor, aunt," answered her
nephew.

The tone of voice arrested her attention.
She looked up in some alarm, saying,

"Has anything happened, Charles?"

"Nothing new, aunt," he answered.
"Will you send your maid away? I want
to speak to you before you leave."

She signed to the woman to quit the room,
and then turned towards her nephew.

"Aunt," he said, going up to her, "I
have sinned against you and against Jeanne.

My only excuse is that when I came back to Lutz I truly thought I came back to die. When life returned I ought to have spoken; but I was so weary of the past, so longing for a little calm and quiet, that I silenced my conscience, thinking no harm could come. I only awoke from my dream three days ago, when Jeanne went to Amonville; then I felt that she had grown so dear to me, life was worthless without her. And I dare not say I love her, aunt, for I am wedded to another woman!"

"Oh! Charles!" exclaimed Madame de Lutz, with mingled indignation and surprise.

"Yes, it is true. Three years ago, in a moment of wild excitement, I married an Italian girl, my inferior in rank. Therefore

I determined to hide my marriage for a time, until I had educated her, and raised her by degrees to the position she was destined to occupy. But I found out my mistake only too soon. Marietta's was not a character to be moulded, and I foresaw such wretchedness for us all if I brought her to Lutz, that I preferred exile for myself. Sickness and death overtook us. Of her own free will she returned to her father's house, and I came home to die, without a regret for life, glad to have done with it. But you and Jeanne mended the broken links, and drew me back to life. You had better have let me go, aunt."

" Why did you not speak then, Charles? Why did you not tell us you had a wife?" said his aunt, bitterly.

"Because I was a coward, and longed for home and peace, at least for a few months. Love was so far from my thoughts, and the weariness of the two years weighed me down to the earth. So I sent Louis to make arrangements for Marietta to remain with her father. I was liberal, and she was content. She does not know my real rank. I had dropped the title of Count when I first went to Italy, and thought it best never to assume it again."

"All wrong! all wrong!" exclaimed Madame de Lutz.

"I know it," he answered sternly. "You cannot judge me more harshly than I do myself."

Madame turned away, longing, yet dreading to speak of Jeanne, her mother's pride forbidding her to suppose that her daughter was wounded. But the Count spoke again, low and sad—

"Aunt, you will take Jeanne to England?"

She faced him then; and he, bowing his head, said simply,

"I love her better than my life!"

"And you have told her so?" she exclaimed, with indignation.

Once more he bowed his head.

"Shame on you, Charles de Lutz!—ten thousand times shame! You are unworthy of your name!" And, drawing herself up to her full height, she left him standing where he was, and went in search of Jeanne.

The Count drew a long, deep sigh, and

then alone retraced his steps to his own solitary home.

Entering Miss Ivor's room, Madame found that Jeanne had gone to bed.

" Mamma !" she exclaimed, " Amie would make me take possession of her bed. I was tired and over-excited, and we were afraid of alarming you. If I can sleep for a couple of hours, I shall be quite ready for our journey."

" My daughter, we will delay our journey till to-morrow," answered Madame. "The Count has just left me, Jeanne."

The blood rushed to Jeanne's face.

" And he has told you, mamma?"

" Yes, Jeanne, he has told me he is a married man, and that he has ventured to speak of love to you."

"Mamma, he could not help it—it was not his fault. Do not ask me more," said Jeanne, clasping her hands, and raising them beseechingly towards her mother.

"It cannot be!" exclaimed Madame de Lutz.

"Mother, it has never ceased to be," answered Jeanne.

"My daughter, you have deceived me too."

"Nay, mother, you would not have had me say I loved him without knowing if his heart were really mine."

"And now, Jeanne?"

"It is a mistake, mother. We will not speak of it," said the girl, hastily. "I was tired and excited—parting with Clotilde, parting from my home. Let me rest to-night. Then take me to England. Afterwards, we will begin life afresh."

She was quite calm ; her manner strangely cold ; she did not, as usual, when even a trifle troubled her, seek a caress from her mother ; her eyes had a strange, startled expression in them, as if she were in pain.

Madame de Lutz took the pale face, and nestled it on her shoulder, saying gently,

"I have brought this on you, Jeanne."

"No, mother, you have ever acted rightly. Do not grieve ; I shall take no harm. I am only startled. Go and rest. Leave me here. To-morrow all will be well."

"You will not come to your own room, Jeanne ?"

"No—I am so tired, I cannot move," was the weary answer. "Take Amie with

you, mamma, and leave me alone; and do
not fret, for I shall be all right to-morrow."

Her mother saw she needed, almost
craved for solitude; and so, smoothing the
hair back from her brow, and kissing her
tenderly, she and Miss Ivor left the room
together. A sigh of relief escaped Jeanne
as she saw the door close on her mother.
Then stealthily she rose, slipped the bolt,
placed with trembling hands the lamp on a
little table beside her bed, felt in the pocket
of her dress for the packet, then lay down
again, and buried her face in the pillows.
But not long did she lie thus. Rousing
herself, she broke the seal, and read a date
three days old; then followed:—

"Jeanne, why did you leave me, and
thus break my dream? The desolation of

your absence is so great that I have awoke
to a great fear. It cannot, may not be that
I should love you! Back to Italy—back
to my chain I must go. Would I had never
laid it down—would you had let me die!
But this is no time for idle regrets. I must
leave you; my very love has pronounced
the decree. Farewell, my gentle Jeanne—
the very essence of purity and womanly
sweetness—thy like I shall never meet
again. You grew long years beside me,
and I was blind; light came to me too late.
Oh! Jeanne, my lesson has been dearly
bought. Even as I write, I seem to see
you, the night of your first ball, floating
past me, with your wreath of rose-buds and
your white dress, pure and simple like
yourself, hiding a woman's true heart and

noble nature. Oh! Jeanne, pardon me my proud blindness! I asked you to be my wife, and refused you what you, with your true instinct, rightly judged was alone worth having—my love. It is yours now; you have conquered, but too late—too late! Oh! child, how often have those words been uttered with wild despair, but never with more bitterness, with deeper sadness, than I write them now! I may not even tell you that I love you.

"You must never know until years hence, when, as the happy wife of another, with children climbing round your knee, you will hear that your cousin, the Count de Lutz, has died in some distant country, and left you his heiress. That is my only comfort, Jeanne, to think that a child of yours will enliven the old Château, making a home of it instead of a stately pile. And then, turning over the papers in my secretary, you will find this. Read, and judge me gently, Jeanne, for the love I bear you. I have erred—but who shall say where the root of the error lies ?

" You and your mother have been fighting against a national institution—a national evil—a thing which is the curse of our land, but which nothing, save a complete revolution in society, can change. In the main you were right. There is something ignoble, revolting, in a woman who gives herself to a man unloving and unloved. But enough ; I cannot enter upon that now. To what purpose ?—it would not restore my lost happiness. Read, then, Jeanne ;

and if you are old, try to remember our youth—be a girl again.

" Do you recollect the first time I went to Rome, how full I was of my art—how determined I was to leave no stone unturned to gain for myself an artist's name? I felt, or thought I felt, the power within me. My original idea had been to go to Rome after our marriage. I knew you would not interfere with my career, engrossing my attention, rivalling my art—pardon me, Jeanne—as another woman would have done. But when I found this marriage was not to be, I determined for two years to lead a purely artistic life. With this intention I left Lutz, you weeping your child-like tears, I dreaming my artist's dream.

" Arrived at Rome, there came a pause.

Only those can understand what I mean who
have visited the Eternal City. There is
something overpowering when one treads
for the first time the city of the Cæsars,
teeming with memories, the past mingling
with the present, the antique with the
modern, heathendom with Christianity. But
not now can I tell you of all this, Jeanne—
as I write, our own individuality absorbs
every other feeling. Would to God I had
never seen Rome!—that I had never trodden
the marble floors of St. Peter's, or gazed on
the turbid waters of the Tiber. After the
first sensation of novelty was over, I began
to think of carrying out my plans. My idea
was to enter any Italian artist's family, to
live their life; and though by this means
freed from all outside cares and the neces-

sity of mixing in society, I might still not feel myself entirely isolated from the world. While ruminating how to accomplish this, circumstances favoured me, and almost without my interference matters were arranged. It happened thus. One afternoon I was riding up and down the Corso; it was the fashionable hour, and more than usually crowded. Arrived at the corner of the Via Condotti, my attention was attracted to a priest. A priest is such a common sight in Rome, that I should doubtless never have looked at him a second time, had it not been for the wan, worn look on his face; indeed he appeared so ill, I wondered to see him standing there, apparently alone. However, I passed on; but returning a second time, I saw my priest attempting to cross the

Corso. Had I not myself drawn back, I must of necessity have ridden over him; as it was, he stumbled and fell. In a second I had dismounted, and throwing my horse's bridle over one arm. with the other I lifted up the fallen man. Fortunately the Corso is very narrow, and he had only taken a few steps off the pavement; but the crowd of equipages and horses is so great at this hour that even this attempt of mine was attended with considerable danger, and caused the bystanders to look on with no little interest. I gave my horse in charge to one of the many loungers, and half supported, half carried the priest into a neighbouring shop, for he had fallen into a dead faint, which lasted some time. When he came to himself, and learnt that I was his preserver, he

was profuse in his thanks, begging earnestly
to know the name of the person to whom
he was indebted for his life. I made light
of the matter, gave him my card, and finding I could be of no further use, withdrew,
and remounting my horse, continued my
ride.

" The following morning, at an early hour,
Louis came into my room and announced
two visitors, the Padre and the Signor
Rocco. In the former I recognised at once
my priest of the day before, and the like-
ness was so strong between the two men
that I needed not the similarity of name to
tell me they were brothers. The only real
difference lay in the tonsured head and close-
shaven face of the priest, and the flowing
hair, somewhat thickly sprinkled with grey,

the full moustache and beard of the artist;
for that he was an artist was evident at the
first glance. They were both tall, handsome men, of the pure Roman type. Fine,
clearly-marked features, and black, piercing
eyes; they were no longer young—past
fifty. I judged the Padre to be the elder of
the two, notwithstanding 'that the Signor
stooped slightly, and had a more settled,
careworn look.

"The Padre had quite recovered from his
indisposition of the previous day, and after
once more thanking me for my timely
assistance, explained that he was subject to
these fainting-fits—that, unfortunately, he
had been called out suddenly to visit a
dying woman; that he had already reached
the corner of the Via Condotti, when he

felt his incapacity to proceed further ; that,
unwilling to disappoint his penitent, he had
nevertheless persevered, with what result I
had seen. But for me he would doubtless
have been killed. ' My brother is ever
thus,' said the Signor. ' When he has an
object in view, nothing stays him ; he would
sooner die than yield, even to bodily weakness.'

" By degrees we conversed on different
subjects—of Rome, and art, the common
talk of all men there ; but when the Signor
learnt that I desired to take my place in
the rank of artists, he expanded—offered to
conduct me to the galleries, and to some
private collections then on view. I willingly accepted, and we started at once, spend-
ing a very pleasant day together. The

Signor consenting to dine with me, I was enabled to explain my future plans to him, asking his advice, and whether he could not recommend me an Italian family of his acquaintance. '*Si! si!*' he answered, after listening to me attentively—'I will think it over—let you know.'

" The following morning the Padre made his appearance, and after some hesitation proposed the following plan. He told me that his brother, the Signor Rocco, occupied a large apartment in the Via Gregoriana; his wife had died the previous year of a malignant fever, which had attacked the whole household. After the Signora's death, half the rooms had been shut up. 'We did not need them, only my brother, myself, and the child Marietta, the one in his studio, the other at his altar, and with his people; besides, there was the expense. Death, illness, and the long-after inaction had undermined the Signor's funds; his school of art had been broken up, and only of late had he been able to re-organise it.'

"The Padre then proceeded to propose to me the occupation of the long-discarded rooms. They were wholly at my service, he said, and, at the same time, I should be able to avail myself of the Signor's artistic advice. The thing seemed just what I wanted, and I immediately proposed visiting the Via Gregoriana. On our way the Padre was careful to inform me that the rooms had been well fumigated, papered, and re-painted, and that I need not fear infection. I assured him I had no such fear, and perfectly trusted him.

"Arrived at the house, we ascended to the upper story by a wide, stately stone staircase, with many doors on every landing, showing it to be inhabited by numerous families. On the top story, however, there was only one door, and a certain stillness seemed to pervade the atmosphere; and when the Padre, making use of his latchkey, admitted us into a sort of ante-room, we seemed to pass into quite another world, so calm, so still.

"Our first visit was to the Signor in his studio, when I at once became aware that he was a man of no ordinary talent, and one under whom I might be proud to study. Afterwards we surveyed the apartments destined for my use. No need to describe them; they consisted of three rooms, salon, atelier, and bedroom. I was content, and agreed to occupy them as soon as a few necessary changes had been effected.

" In a couple of days I found myself established in my new quarters. It had been settled that I should take my meals with the family, which I had understood to con· sist of the Padre, the Signor, and a little girl, whom the Padre always spoke of as ' the child Marietta.' Judge, then, of my surprise when, the first time I took my place at table, I saw opposite me one of the most beautiful women I had ever seen. She was alike perfect in form and face. It needed no artist's eye to appreciate her beauty—it was self-evident. I have seen

many lovely women in nature as in art,
but never have I met with Marietta's rival.
My face must have betrayed my admiration,
for, as the maiden bowed her head in recog-
nition of my presence, I remember well the
rich deep colour which mantled her cheek
and brow. She still wore mourning for her
mother—a plain black dress, fitting tight to
her exquisitely-moulded form; no ornament, no jewel marred the simplicity; and,
in truth, she needed none—she was herself
a jewel of Nature's own making.

"I will not dwell upon that fatal beauty,
Jeanne. It is enough you understand.
Days and weeks glided on—I worked hard
and well; nothing disturbed me. Marietta
I only saw at meal times; but, alas! I learnt
to look upon those hours as the best, the

happiest in the day. It was a delight to sit opposite and gaze from time to time upon her beauty. It was a feast of itself—an epicure's feast, which never for one moment palled upon my taste, Her father and uncle were both proud of her after their fashion ; but they paid little or no attention to the motherless girl. She lived a life perfectly apart from ours, with only her old nurse, Teresa, for friend and companion.

"It was from Teresa I learnt that Marietta's mother had been a common peasant girl from the Campagna—that seeing her one day selling fruit upon the market-place, the Signor Rocco had been struck with her marvellous beauty, and had sought to obtain her for a model, but the girl's parents had refused. Whether through cunning, or in the ordinary course of events, the Signor had by degrees been so drawn on, that at last he asked and obtained the peasant girl for his wife. 'He lived to rue the day,' said Teresa, in conclusion ; 'she never loved him, only married him from ambition ; and what with her jealousy, fierce temper, and poor relations, the Signor has had a hard life of it. As for the child, I believe the mother was jealous of its beauty from the time she weaned her to her dying day. I never saw her caress her as other mothers do their little ones. The Signor would have sent her to the convent, and had her taught, but his wife would not hear of it.' ' What, make her daughter wiser than herself, that she might scorn her mother ! No, she should not go, but stay at home and learn to help Teresa.' 'So, but for the Padre, her uncle, Marietta had not so much as learnt to read.'

"Thus, Jeanne, something more was added to the charm of Marietta's beauty—namely, pity. Pity for the lovely girl growing up in such perfect loveliness between those two old men. She never went out, save to early mass, before the rest of the household was astir, when Teresa accompanied her, who, with her large market-basket, profited by the occasion to do her day's marketing.

"I sometimes found myself wondering how Marietta bore her solitary existence. She seemed to stand in great awe both of her father and uncle, and seldom spoke to any one. I do not suppose I exchanged a dozen phrases with her in the course of the first three months.

"At last, one day, seeing some choice flowers during my afternoon's stroll, I purchased them, brought them home, and laid them by Marietta's plate at dinner. I cannot describe her astonishment and delight. Her gratitude for so small a gift showed me how entirely uncared for and unspoilt the girl had been. From henceforth never a day passed but what Marietta had her flowers. It was reward enough for me to see the beautiful face brighten up and glow with pleasure. Her father and uncle were always present, and showed almost as much astonishment and gratitude as Marietta herself. One day, however, I had procured for her a bunch of most lovely roses—they were beautiful even

for Rome, where flowers are so abundant—
but instead of, as usual, laying them beside
her, I placed them in a vase in the centre
of the table. Great was the general admiration bestowed upon them, but Marietta
said never a word, and avoided looking at
me. Once, however, I saw her beautiful
eyes rest upon the flowers, full to overflowing with tears. The meal was half over,
when I turned carelessly to the Signor,
saying, 'Signor, I have two favours to ask
you, may I count upon your granting them?'
'Most assuredly, if within my power,' he
answered, courteously. 'The first is, then,'
I replied, 'to permit me to make a sketch
of your daughter; and the second is, that,
feeling disinclined for work to-day, I have
ordered a carriage to take me to Tivoli, and

should esteem it a favour if you and the Padre would accompany me, and also persuade the Signorina to break through her seclusion for one afternoon.' The Roman dearly loves a holiday, and I saw that my proposition gave satisfaction. The Signor answered. smiling, 'As for the sketch, I give my consent; Marietta is now the person to decide whether she is willing. You will find it troublesome, Signor; I never take amateur models.' 'Merely for a sketch,' I interposed.' ' Well, well, you will settle it between you. As to Tivoli, I think we are all agreed that it will be a pleasant excursion.' And so, without further discussion, the matter was settled, and an hour later we were on our way to those far-famed gardens.

" It was such a rare holiday for Marietta, and she looked so radiantly beautiful sitting opposite me in the carriage. As we drove through the town I became aware that she attracted considerable attention. Arrived at Hadrian's Villa, we left the carriage at the gate, and began strolling through the grounds. Jeanne, child, you cannot imagine the effect of that climate, of those scenes, on certain temperaments. It is something enervating, overpowering. It seemed to me as if I were dreaming some strange, intoxicating dream, wandering thus, with Marietta beside me, through long avenues of trees, amidst ruins of vast temples and ancient theatres, up banks laden with flowers, the air around us heavy with perfume, and the sky above one ethereal blue. It was

one of those dreamy days in which one lives
for the moment only, caring neither for the
past nor for the future. No word was exchanged between Marietta and myself which
the whole world might not have heard,
only I obtained her promise that she would
sit for me to make a sketch of her face.
That night, on our return, I took my vase
of roses, and giving them to Teresa, bade
her place them in the Signorina's room. On
a slip of paper I had written the words,
'In remembrance of Tivoli!' From that day
forth, I hardly know how, it was so gradual,
the tone of my intercourse with Marietta entirely changed in character. I did not see
her oftener alone; true, I took the desired
sketch, but it was in her father's atelier. Her
words were few, but her looks and her

gestures warned me that we were both playing a hazardous game.

"Why uselessly linger over the tale?
You guess how it was. Day by day I grew
more deeply entranced with Marietta's
beauty, and day by day she grew to love
me with all the passion of her Italian
nature. I could feel her glance follow me
as I moved about the room—that mellow,
speaking glance which rouses all our passions. So Marietta fascinated me, and I
never paused to ask myself whither we
were tending, until, one morning, the Padre
came into my atelier, looking grave and
anxious, and after examining my work for
some time, said, 'My brother and myself
are much troubled, Signor.' 'Ah!' I said,
'and wherefore?—has anything happened?'

'It is about Marietta,' he answered. 'Indeed!' I said, continuing my painting— 'what has the Signorina done?' 'She has refused to marry a most estimable youth,' was the answer, 'an artist, like her father, the Signor Antonio. You have seen him in the atelier. The young man has a little property, and is well to do; it is a good match. Marietta must be mad.' 'Has she given any reason for her refusal?' I asked. 'None, save a flood of tears, and an entreaty not to force her—that the Signor Antonio was not pleasing to her—as if the girl knew what sort of man would make a good husband! This is what comes of having no mother. If the Signora Rocco had been alive, Marietta would not have dared to utter a dissenting word; now we are at

a loss. What do you recommend, Signor?'
'To leave her alone, Padre, and she will
come round. Try to force a woman, and
you only make her obstinate.' '*Si! si!* I
think you have hit the mark, Signor. I
will tell my brother, and persuade Signor
Antonio to patience;' and therewith he left
my atelier. But the impetus to thought
had been given, and for the first time I
asked myself what my intentions with re-
gard to Marietta were. I knew she was no
wife for me. I could not bring her home,
and place her beside you and my aunt as
the Countess de Lutz; yet Marietta loved
me, and might well interpret into a similar
feeling my admiration. I threw down my
paint-brushes impatiently, and taking up my
hat, sallied forth.

" Passing by the Piazza di Spagna, I
stood for a moment gazing at the numerous
models lying in all sorts of positions, in
every variety of costume, the whole length
of the steps. There were some beautiful
women in the different groups, but I sought
in vain for one worthy to stand beside
Marietta. Turning away, I entered the
Accademia di Francia, and stretching myself on a bench, took myself seriously to
task, and at last decided upon a course of
action which would react upon Marietta.

" I did not make my reappearance at the
Via Gregoriana till the next morning at the
late breakfast. As I took my usual seat, I
looked across at Marietta. Her eyes were
bent, and the long dark silken lashes swept
her cheek; the usually bright colour had

quite faded ; she looked pale and careworn —those few hours had changed her strangely. Seeing her thus, I felt that, unless I spoke at once, my own courage would surely fail me ; so, turning to Signor Rocco, I said—' I am much annoyed at being obliged to leave Rome immediately for an indefinite time, but I received last night letters from France which require my return without delay. I regret the interruption in my studies, but am forced to submit to circumstances.'

" This was true, Jeanne. The bank at Amonville had just failed, and my presence, if not absolutely necessary, was desirable, and proved most useful, as you know. Both the Padre and Signor were loud in their regrets, assuring me that my apartment should be kept in readiness against my return. I thanked them warmly, and told them my departure was fixed for the next day—that Louis was already packing my things.

" During our conversation, Marietta never once lifted her eyes—she seemed not even to hear—not a look could I obtain from her ; but her pale face spoke to my heart far more eloquently than words. Only once, when I announced my departure for the next day, I saw all her features quiver, as with suppressed pain. Disinclined to work, irritated, and ill at ease, I left the house late that afternoon, and wandered carelessly about, through narrow back-streets, utterly indifferent where I went, till sud denly, and without knowing it, I found myself at the foot of the Capitol. It was evening now—near upon sunset, and, returning on my footsteps, I became conscious of two muffled figures close behind me. I should have passed on without further notice, but something familiar in the graceful bearing of the taller of the two attracted my attention. I paused, and looked more steadily at them. In another minute I recognised Marietta, and was at her side. 'Marietta, what are you doing here at this time of night?' I asked. 'I have come to bid you farewell,' she answered, in her sweet, musical voice. 'But not here,' I replied; 'surely not here.' 'And wherefore not?' she answered. 'What spot more appropriate for a Roman maiden to bid farewell to her lover than her own Capitol—

' but, ah ! I forgot,' she continued, speaking quickly, 'there is one other place still better suited, where woman's trust and weakness met with their reward, crushed mercilessly beneath men's iron shields. Lend me your arm, Signor, for I am weary, and I will guide you thither.'

" I did as she bade me, for her manner awed me. Never before had I heard her speak in that tone, breathing alike pride and passion. I took her hand, and placed it on my arm, without speaking. Then we both moved quickly on, Teresa following at a discreet distance. An Italian woman loves an intrigue, and Teresa belonged thoroughly to her class and nation. Up the great flight of steps, past the statues of Castor and Pollux, and the mutilated form

of Marcus Aurelius, all shadowy in the growing shades of evening, we passed rapidly;
then down a narrow street, until we stopped
at a gate. A piece of money given to the
gate-keeper, a word to Teresa, bidding
her await our return, and once more we
moved rapidly on. I could not stay Marietta's steps, until we stood together on the
brow of the Tarpeian rock, overlooking all
the north part of Rome and the distant
Campagna.

" 'Now,' she said, throwing back her veil,
and stretching out her hand towards me,
' now I will say addio.' Her great black
eyes were flashing out upon me like two
stars gleaming in the darkness.

" There are moments in our existence
when we cease to be ourselves, when all that

is true and noble in our natures seems suddenly overwhelmed, submerged, and passions, the very subtlest in our being, rise up and hold us in subjection, unless by some mighty effort we can cast them off. How rarely, alas! does one come forth unscathed from such a combat!

"That lovely June night I knew not that the moon was shining and the stars had risen when we retraced our steps, and found Teresa impatiently awaiting us at the postern gate.

"'Ah! what will the Signor say, Marietta, when he misses us?' was the hurried greeting. 'He will not miss us,' answered Marietta, shortly. 'He has an engagement, and will not be home till late.'

"Then, once more wrapping her veil

around her, and now leaning on my arm, we turned homewards. It was a long distance, and I thought she must be weary, so asked her gently, ‘Marietta, shall I call a vettura?’ She lifted her head, and I felt her lean more heavily upon me as she murmured, ‘And so shorten our last hour together.’ ‘Nay, nay.’ So we went on ; nor paused until we reached the Fontana di Trevi. There Marietta stopped of her own accord, and, leaving my arm, passed round to where there was a small opening in the balustrade. The white moonlight was pouring down upon the streams of foaming water gushing out from the huge horses’ mouths like glistening silver ; while bearded Neptune, holding high his trident, looked down upon the scene.

" 'Come, come,' said Marietta, impatiently, signing for me to advance to her side.
At the same moment she stooped, and filling the palms of her hands with water, held
them up to my lips, saying, ' Drink, drink
quickly,' and I obeyed. 'Now you will
come back,' she said, breathing a long sigh
of relief, ' I know you will. The Fontana
never lies.' It is a Roman legend, he who
drinks of the Fontana di Trevi is sure to
come back to Rome.

" Once more we moved on ; but Marietta
had ceased weeping now, and walked with
a lighter step. Arrived at the corner of the
Via Condotti, she held out her hand, saying,
' Here we part, *Addio, ed a rivederti, caro
mio.* Each morning and each night I will
pray the Blessed Virgin for you, and await

your return. Now, do not follow me.'

"Thus speaking, she disappeared round the corner, followed by Teresa. The next morning I left Rome for Lutz. At that moment I loved Marietta with one of those subtle passions which, when it takes possession of a man, blinds him to all else save the pleasure of the hour. Our nature is twofold—it has its coarser and its finer elements. Some women appeal only to the former, and by them alone hold us in sway; but with a man worthy of the name their power rarely lasts —passion is followed by satiety, and the links are broken.

"When I left Rome my passion for Marietta was still too fresh for me to feel this. Had I remained, I know now that it must have been so; but we parted almost before I had realized the fact that I was loved. The charm was new, and lingered round me like a pleasant dream, which I was never weary of recalling. On my journey homeward I reviewed my situation, and determined at once to carry out my uncle's wishes, and conclude the marriage he had arranged. I never for one moment anticipated opposition from you, nor from my aunt, at this my second demand. You would fulfil your duty, I should accomplish . mine, and Marietta would sink into a memory, a regret. What man had not experienced the same? I reasoned that I should differ in nothing from others. It was in this frame of mind that I came amongst you, and found my aunt as unreasonable, from my point of view, as

ever. It irritated me. What right had
she to sound the depths of my feelings?
Other men took wives, caring for them far
less than I cared for you! Besides, you
belonged to me, I had waited for you, no
other human being had a right to lay his
hand upon you. I remember the idea cross-
ing me once that Gordon was seeking to
win you, and I accused your mother of en-
couraging him. I was angered, I scarcely
knew why or wherefore; it was as if an in-
justice were being perpetrated upon me. On
the same day I asked you to be my wife, and
you refused. I have had an inkling since of
what you were waiting for, Jeanne. I have
thought within the last few days how I might
have wooed you gently to me by one word
of love. Alas! I would not recognize the

fact that the child had become the woman. You seemed cold to me, and doubtless I seemed so to you. How could it be otherwise, coming, as I did, freighted with passion from that land of passion, with the image of Marietta, and her marvellous beauty, haunting me, and making all things else look tame and shallow in comparison? Knowing what I had left behind me for duty's sake, and seeing myself rejected, I craved after the forbidden fruit, as an accustomed opium-eater craves after the forbidden morsel. Your mother was right—I did not love you; and had you been my wife, I doubt whether we should have been happy. Our love would never have developed; the image of that other woman would have come between you and me. But enough;

wherever the wrong lay, we cannot undo it
now. It seems to me, looking back, as if
at this time all things combined to drive
me to the very place I ought, of all others,
to have avoided. It is difficult for me to
relate the next event which bore upon my
life, because it is always difficult for a man
to cast the least reflection upon one of the
opposite sex; yet I cannot pass it over in
silence, and time will have mellowed all
things when you read this.

"Louise de la Croix had only been married a few months when I met her at the
ball your mother gave at the Château. Do
you remember, Jeanne? She was young
and beautiful, careless and gay; she had
been thrown, utterly without preparation,
into the vortex of Parisian society. Her

husband left her perfect and entire freedom, glad to buy his own liberty on such easy terms. Marriage with him, as with most men of his class, had been merely a matter of calculation. His fortune required repairs before it was too seriously damaged, and he required an heir to perpetuate the family name. The former Louise's wealth assured him, the latter he had every reason to believe would follow in due course of time. But, beyond this, a wife was an encumbrance to him. Not for any woman in the world would he have altered the even tenor of his life; he never dreamt of doing so, and after the first month of matrimony Louise was perfectly aware that she was her own mistress, entirely and completely independent. She was rich; she was

young; she was beautiful. Naturally men
gathered round her, flattering and exalting
her to the skies; she saw daily, hourly,
other women, holding their heads high, and
moving the queens of society, whom she
learnt in a few weeks to recognise as faithless wives and mothers—women whose
only object it was to observe the outward
forms of decency—who, had they borne
other names—had the glitter of gold not
created a sort of aureole around them—
would have been pointed at by the finger
of scorn, and every door closed in their
faces.

"Doubtless—in fact, I know it—the Marquise shrunk at first from this state of
things, and kept herself aloof. But habit,
alas! is second nature; the edge of her

conscience was blunted by degrees; she had many adorers, but no especial *preux chevalier*, like all the other ladies of her society—no one addicted to her service above all others, and she felt aggrieved. There could be no harm in that—it was useful, agreeable; he would fulfil the thousand little nothings so necessary to a woman's comfort, and which her husband utterly ignored. Such was her frame of mind when she came to Lutz, and her eye fell on me. I was single, an old acquaintance, a man who had never given occasion for gossip—in fact, a safe man; so she threw herself somewhat in my way, and drew me to her house. She meant no harm at first; she felt sure of her own honourable intentions; she was only amusing her-

self. But I did not meet her half-way.
The position she would have had me assume
has ever seemed to me the lowest, the
vilest a man can stoop to.

" By degrees rumours, courteous congratulations, respecting my *liaison* with the Marquise, reached me from more than one quarter.
How they got wing I cannot tell, but I determined speedily to close the mouths of men
once and for all. In four-and-twenty hours
after taking the briefest adieux, I left Paris
for Rome. I did not care to return to
Lutz, and the moth will hover round the
candle until its wings are singed. I reasoned that, though in Rome, I need not see
Marietta. I knew how seldom she went
out—how easy, therefore, it would be to
avoid her. A school-boy might have rea-

soned as wisely—I know it now, but I did not see it then. I think there are moments in every man's life when he is mentally blind as regards his own feelings, and perfectly incapable of justly weighing the importance of his own actions. I doubt even if another can open his eyes. We must each and all buy our own experience; it was even so with me.

"For one month, however, true to my resolution, I religiously avoided the Via Gregoriana; only at night, sometimes, I would walk slowly along on the other side of the street, and gaze upwards at Marietta's window, hoping to see, if it were but her shadow. Once or twice I succeeded in doing so, and went home reasoning against reason—that there could be no possible harm in my presenting my addresses to the family in general. Through Louis I learnt that Marietta was not married.

"I had been about six weeks in Rome, when Louis came into my room one morning earlier than usual; he fidgeted about for some time, and at last said abruptly, 'Monsieur will be angry, I fear, but as I was passing by the Chiesa della Trinità this morning, I saw Teresa coming down the steps, with the Signorina leaning on her arm. They had seen me before I was aware of it, and Teresa, calling out to me, obliged me to remain and greet them. The Signorina was just as white as a sheet, Monsieur le Comte; she did not speak a word, and I think she would have fallen to the ground, had it not been for the support of

Teresa's strong arm, who explained to me
eagerly that the young lady had been ill,
very ill, near unto death—that she was now
only just able to crawl about, but that she
would drag herself to the Blessed Virgin's
altar night and morning, kneeling before
the shrine until she almost dropped from
exhaustion. "Ah! it is cruel—cruel!" she
exclaimed; adding, "And so you and your
master are back in Rome, Signor Louis, and
have forgotten your old friends. Truly the
French are a volatile people; their memories cannot extend over six months;" and
as she spoke, her piercing black eyes looked
at me indignantly. I ventured to say we
had only arrived lately, were but passing
through Rome on our way south, but that I
doubted not Monsieur le Comte would pay

his respects to the family before leaving.
She hardly seemed to believe me, shook
her head doubtingly, and muttering something in Italian to the Signorina, nodded to
me, and passed on.'

"I had listened in silence, but not without emotion. What he told me concerning
Marietta moved me to the quick. I, however, only asked if he had given my ad-
dress; and being answered in the negative,
desired him to leave me. Once alone, my
thoughts flew to Marietta. Had she been
pining thus for me?—had I in reality so
wounded her heart as to change the beautiful bright girl into the sickly, ailing woman,
who day by day dragged her weak limbs to
the Virgin's shrine, there to pray for the
return of her beloved? And for thirty

days I had been within a stone's-throw of her, indifferent to her sufferings, careless, though she might be dying, when a single word, a look, would have gladdened her!

" I hesitated now no longer. That very day I would seek Marietta. If I could only wait patiently till the evening, I was sure of finding her alone; the Signor and Padre would both be at their cafés. So I waited wearily. The hours that day seemed weighted with lead. Remember, it was the first time I had ever felt the charm—the full power of being loved entirely, exclusively, as I believed Marietta loved me; for you, Jeanne, have no idea what Italian women are, especially of Marietta's standing. Uneducated, unguided, save by priests and superstition, they have no employment, no mental culture, and live but for one thing—love. When it comes to them, their whole nature expands, and goes forth to meet it ; they never hesitate ; they never think.   An Italian woman gives herself up wholly and entirely to her passion, neither counting the cost, nor regretting it when paid.   Love constitutes their being ; it knows no rival ; they live in and for it.   To realise aright the loves of Romeo and Juliet, we must tread their land and breathe its atmosphere. And I knew that such a woman was waiting for me even then—one to whom I alone could bring sunlight and joy—to whom my presence was light, my absence almost death.   No marvel, then, if my whole soul went forth in gratitude to the woman who could thus think and feel for me.   Friend-

ship, affection, I had known; but love—
never until this day.

"Evening came at last, and once more
I ascended the great stone staircase and
stopped at the door of Marietta's home. A
moment I hesitated, as one involuntarily
does at every great crisis of his life. It is
as if an invisible hand were laid upon us,
bidding us pause ere we risk our all. Then I
knocked a low knock and waited—a minute,
and I heard Teresa's shuffling walk along
the corridor. She turned the lock; I
entered. She would have screamed aloud
in her Italian excitability, but I placed my
finger on my lips in token of silence, and
whispered in her ear, 'Marietta.' She answered with a shake of the head, and tears
rising in her still bright black eyes, while

she pointed towards a little room, which I knew was Marietta's habitual retreat. It opened out of Teresa's, and was more shabbily furnished than the rest of the house. I followed the direction indicated, and quietly, without knocking, opened the door. It was growing dark. A few embers on the hearth faintly lighted the room, and showed its only ornament, a large and exquisite picture of the Mother and Child. On a low, quaintly-carved *prie-dieu*, placed fronting the hearth, knelt Marietta, her head raised, her eyes fixed on the Madonna, while from between her clasped fingers the beads of a rosary dropped one by one.

"Yes, Jeanne, you see it now. My picture of 'Waiting" was a life-picture. My entrance was unheard. The suppliant did not stir, but continued her devotions, her lips moving silently. Even in that half-light I saw how changed she was. The glow of health had faded from her cheeks, her hands looked long and thin, and there was the lassitude of despair in the bowed attitude of the graceful figure. It needed but a minute to see all this; then, in a low voice, I said, 'Marietta!' She started, turned, saw me standing, made one step towards me, stopped short, turned her head towards the Madonna, signed herself, murmured, 'Grazie, Madonna mia!' and the next instant was lying in my arms.

"I will pass over the following hour. What can I tell you, save that the passionate love of this woman intoxicated me? Had I never woke up, had I died then, it would have been well for her and me. How the time passed I know not, but suddenly we were roused by hearing footsteps in the corridor. We thought it was Teresa, and did not stir, but in another minute facing us stood the Padre. I can scarcely recall the angry words which passed between us, words the like of which I had not borne, save from a man of his class. He attempted to take Marietta out of my arms, where she lay sobbing wildly. 'To-night she shall be hidden in the convent,' said the Padre. 'Better that my brother should return to a childless rather than a dishonoured home.' 'I will not go,' cried Marietta, springing up and facing her uncle. 'I will follow him, my heart's delight! You shall not part us. Has not the Madonna given him back to me?

Have I not prayed day and night to win him ? Thou shalt not part us, I say !'

" 'Foolish girl,' answered the priest, shrugging his shoulders, ' thou thinkest he loves thee ! Ask him to make thee his wife, and see then what his love is worth ! And yet I tell thee thou must be his wife to-night, or to-morrow, at dawn of day, the convent gates close on thee and thy dishonour for ever. Thou knowest me, thou knowest my power ; now plead with thy lover.'

" He spoke scoffingly, and, as he did so, moved away to the further end of the room; and, before I could answer him, Marietta was lying white as marble, prone to the ground at my feet. ' Oh ! forsake me not, forsake me not !' she cried, in her passionate Italian. ' Consign me not to a living tomb !

Give me but the name of wife, and I will serve thee as no woman ever served man before.'

"She would have said still more, but I raised her, and holding her in my arms, sought to comfort her. I knew well the powers of the Church at Rome, and I knew the Padre both could and would fulfil his threat. To save Marietta at any cost, that was my only thought. 'Lead on, Signore Padre,' I said haughtily. 'Marietta shall not be consigned to a convent. Go and prepare your altar. In an hour she shall be my wife.'

"He turned and looked at me with a stupefied air of astonishment. A minute's silence; then, seeing I did not move, nor utter another word, 'Follow me,' he said.

We did so, Marietta clinging to me. Her momentary strength had left her; she was weeping now like a terrified child. 'Hush, hush, Marietta, all is well. No one shall harm you at my side.' Thus I sought to cheer and re-assure her, as, preceded by the Padre, and followed by Teresa, we descended the staircase, passed along the dimly-lighted street, and mounted the steps leading to the Monte della Trinità. With the conflicting passions of love, anger, and pity warring within me, I still knew what I was doing—I knew that I was sealing my fate for life, my misery perhaps. As I entered the church your father's face arose before me, sad and earnest, even as I had known and loved it in life; but Marietta, in all her marvellous, luring beauty, was clinging to

my arm. Through the dim church we followed the dark form of the Padre, until we
stood before the grating which separated us
from the high altar. Taking a small key
from his pocket, the priest opened the iron
gate, passed through, and signed to us to do
the same. All was dark and still. No
sound broke the silence, and the sacred lamp
swinging above the altar alone cast a pale,
wavering light over the scene. There, according to the rights of the Romish Church,
Marietta and I were made man and wife !"

CHAPTER XI.

" I HAVE not much more to tell. Coming out of the church, my resolution
was at once taken. I would leave Rome
that very night, taking Marietta with me,
and for a time, at least, our marriage should
be kept secret, until, by force of association
and education, Marietta should have grown
up to her new position. Standing therefore
on the steps, I turned quickly and haughtily
to the Padre, saying shortly, ' Marietta is
now my wife, and will follow me. Addio !'
I gave him no time for opposition, but half-

carrying Marietta, hurried her into a carriage,
and drove straight to my hotel. Bidding
Louis pack, I arranged everything for our
immediate departure, and before midnight
we were on our way to Naples. In the
environs of that beautiful city I took a villa.
Retired, hidden from all the world, we lived
for five months. But long ere that time
had elapsed I knew that I had bound myself to a woman who, beyond her perfect
beauty, and her passionate love for me, had
not one thought, one idea in common with
myself; and as her reserve wore off, and we
grew accustomed to each other, I found her
develop into just the same woman Teresa
had told me her mother had been. She
could not endure my having anything, even
an idea, apart from her; she was jealous of

my art, she was jealous of my books. I
sufficed to her existence, and she felt she
ought to complete mine; but, alas! she
could not! Day by day the fact grew
plainer and plainer, and the breach widened
between us. In vain I strove to heal it, and
for a-while succeeded, lulling myself to rest
with the delusion that time and association
would draw us closer together, and make
unlike like.

"It was now that I painted my famous
picture of 'Waiting.' Marietta was a good
model. and the employment suited her. It
needed no exertion, kept me occupied with
her alone; and she asked nothing better than
to kneel thus before me hours together.

"Have you ever on a very cold day suddenly entered a hot-house? The heat is

pleasant at first, and seems to penetrate
and warm the whole body ; but after the
first ten minutes a feeling of lassitude, almost
of suffocation, follows. Air—fresh, free air
—one must have at any cost ; that artificial
atmosphere becomes unbearable. · One hur-
ries out, drawing a long breath, glad to feel
the clear fresh air ; even though it make one
shiver, at least it is life.

" A sensation something akin to this was
gradually, but surely, creeping over me in
my Neapolitan villa. A restlessness, a wild
longing for change, drove me forth at times.
I thought of Lutz, I thought of you all with
strange, eager desire ; but I was less willing
than ever to bring Marietta amongst you.
If I absented myself for an hour or two, on
my return I was sure to be greeted with

bitter reproaches and wild bursts of passion, followed by remorse equally exaggerated. At first I soothed her, as one would a child; then I reasoned gently, kindly; but it was of no avail, and in the long run only made matters worse, so I finished by taking little or no notice of these outbursts.

"Thus time went on, when one day we received the news that the Padre was dying, and desired most earnestly to see us. We hurried to Rome, and arrived just in time to see him in life; but he was unconscious, and recognised neither of us. After his death we still lingered in Rome, and it was at this time that by some means or other Madame de la Croix found me out, and visited me in my atelier. My reception of her was not such as to induce her to return;

but it had the effect of making me decide upon a new course of action.

"To bring Marietta to Lutz would, I felt more than ever persuaded, be entailing misery on us all. I could not have introduced her into society—such a step could only have been productive of humiliation to me, and deep sorrow to my aunt. I determined, therefore, to break off all connection with my home, and to spend the next few years travelling with my wife ; and thus gradually initiate her into the forms of society, by mixing with what should fall in our way, as occasion offered. I arranged my affairs accordingly, writing to my aunt and to my lawyer, making my will, and putting all things in order. Then I informed the Signor Rocco of our immediate departure. The

Signor made some objections to our travelling, which, however, I made light of; and once more we left Rome. This time Teresa accompanied us, for on the eve of our departure Marietta told me she expected to be a mother.

"You may imagine, Jeanne, how this knowledge stirred up once more my dying love for her—how I forced myself to be gentle and patient, bestowing all my time and care to give her pleasure. No whim but what I sought to gratify; she asked but to receive. It was in vain Teresa warned me I was doing wrong. 'You will suffer for it,' she said. 'It was just the same with her mother. You are spoiling her, and she cannot bear it; she will make you pay a heavy penalty.'

"But I would not heed her; I could but believe that once a child upon her bosom, Marietta would learn wisdom, and we should be, if not happy, at least at peace. But I had yet to learn, Jeanne, that Italian women, of Marietta's temperament, are capable of but one feeling—passion. All milder forms of love are as nought to them—they do not satisfy them; they do not comprehend them; and so when Marietta became a mother, instead of a link, the child widened the gap between us. From the hour of its birth, Marietta lived in mortal dread lest my love should pass from her to it. There was not a device she did not practise to hide the child from me. For a time I seemed to ignore the fact, hoping thus to lull her jealousy to

rest; but in vain. It was a girl, Jeannette
—a De Lutz in every feature; and it grew
to be such a bright, merry little thing. I
gave her your name, dear, thinking of the
time when I should bring her home to you,
and you would welcome the mother for the
child's sake.

"I also at this time had my marriage
ratified according to French law, fearful lest
any stain should rest upon my little daughter. This angered Marietta. Why had I
not done so sooner?—why need the child
be considered where she had been neglected? But I had long since ceased to
argue, and let matters take their course. I
need hardly tell you how I loved my baby-
daughter; how she grew daily closer and
closer to my heart—it was all I had left.

Between Marietta and myself love was now but a name—a thing to be wrangled about; and we had never had anything else in common. All my hopes died out one by one. I knew that nothing was left me save to bear the burden I had taken upon myself, the weight of which would have been intolerable to a man of my temperament, save for my art and my little girl's caresses. Oh! the charm of those baby-arms about my neck, those soft baby-kisses! I seem as I write to feel them still. She soon learnt to know me in her little way, and when she caught sight of me would shout for joy, and almost leap out of Teresa's arms to meet me. This angered her mother beyond all bounds, and two or three times harsh words passed between us—harsher words than I had ever thought to utter to a woman.

"So time passed on, I working hard, and winning, as you know, some success. At times I asked myself what my future would be? I could not for ever remain an exile; and yet to take Marietta to Lutz seemed daily less and less desirable. I knew that once passed babyhood, my daughter would require other guidance than her mother's. I need not have troubled myself, for suddenly there broke over our home, such as it was, a storm which laid it low even to the ground. The child sickened with one of those low fevers so common in Italy. We did not think much of it at first; and Marietta laughed at my anxiety. But suddenly she grew worse, and before many hours had elapsed, I held the lifeless body of my child in my arms. Oh! how gladly I would have died in its stead!

"Marietta's loud wailing and boisterous grief were more than I could bear—they seemed a mockery; yet I soothed and calmed her, and after a time persuaded her to take some repose, leaving Teresa to watch beside her; and I—I took up *my watch* beside my dead child, and in those long hours of agony I painted her sleeping her last sleep. It seems to me now, looking back, as if my very life oozed away in the work. How I did it—how I moulded those little hands, lying so listless now—those tiny feet, that would never run to meet me—how I committed to canvas that baby-

face, in all its sleeping beauty, I know not.
Night and day I laboured as one con-
demned to do so. Another will, not my
own, seemed to drive me on; and ever as
I painted, the finger of death grew more
and more visible on my darling. It seemed
as if I and the grave were fighting for the
victory, which of us should hold our own
the longest. It was finished at last; and hiding her beneath flowers as fresh and fragile
as herself, I laid my darling in her last
resting-place. A marble cross above her
head, her name, the date of her birth and
death—sole records of her short and stain-
less life.

"Scarcely had the child been dead a week
when Marietta sickened of the same disease.
For weeks we despaired of her life, watch-

ing night and day beside her. Before she
was fairly out of danger, my turn came.
I was already so weakened that the fever
prostrated me directly; and yet I lived.
Week after week I lay there helpless.
From my room I could hear Marietta's con-
tinual moan and wail—it was hard, very
hard to die away from Rome. At last,
wearied, I asked the doctor what it were
best to do. He said it was a sick whim, a
fancy which it would be well to satisfy.
She was too weak to be reasoned with. If
possible she ought to go home. So, at my
request, he wrote to her father, enclosing
travelling expenses, and bidding him come
and fetch his daughter. Gently I broke it
to Marietta, telling her the doctor ordered
her home. She seemed to have lost all

self-control—her love, her jealousy, everything had disappeared before the terror of
death. Yes, she would go home; and I
should follow her as soon as I recovered—
for of course I should recover—I was a man,
and strong. So when her father came, she
went contentedly, and left me with Louis
for my nurse. I have not seen her since.
I lay long ill—three months, I think; and
then, when I thought death could not be far
off, came home to die; but God willed it
otherwise, and I have lived to love you,
Jeanne, and now I must leave you.

"Oh! how blind we are! I know that in
the future your image alone will haunt me!
You have taken possession of all that is best
and holiest in my nature. Oh! Jeanne,
Jeanne, I shall see you once again, darling,

and then farewell. If I stayed beside you, a word, a look might betray me. A man is not always master of himself; and I would rather die than wound you. Yet how gladly I would read your inmost soul. It is hard to leave you, to know that others may take that which I once neglected, but which now I have learnt to value only too highly."

Jeanne closed the manuscript, and lay back upon her pillows. Who shall say what her thoughts were—how they went and came? A strange mixture of pain and pleasure. The knowledge that she was loved, loved so dearly, made her heart beat with a strange, wild longing. She closed her eyes, and, forgetful of all else, dreamt of that paradise of earthly love, and so she fell asleep. Martyrs and criminals sleep the eve of their execution. God, in His mercy, wills it so! With early morning she awoke, and then the remembrance of the events of the day before came rushing back to her. She closed her eyes again for one minute, as if to shut out the light of day; but not long did she lie thus. Rising, she dressed herself, threw open the window, and stood breathing the fresh morning air. Her brain and heart recovered their balance, acting together—she was herself again; and when, at their usual early breakfast hour, she went into her mother's room, and wished her good morning, few would have guessed that she had fought a great battle with herself, and had come forth victorious.

She knew that from henceforth her life, her love, her all must be hidden away from the world, away from her friend, away even from that much-loved mother, who had nurtured and tended her; it must be hidden down in the very depths of her own heart ; her love! her secret! the hope and joy of her youth! Alas! she ignored, how few of her sex there are who do not bear burdens equal to her own! We grow accustomed to them. sometimes even finish by forgetting their existence, until one day the perfume of a flower, a ray of sunshine, the tone of a voice, a mere nothing, and yet *the thing* awakes the dead, and surges up within, the loves, the memories long since laid to rest.

So, with womanly tact and quickness,

Jeanne recognized and picked up the thread of her life, snapped for one little moment. To screen herself and her cousin, that was her object. Not if she could help it should blame attach to him. None, before her, should speak harshly of his past, or judge his wife. *All* that belonged to him was dear and sacred to her. And therefore, when her mother, coming towards her, spoke softly, caressingly, desirous, yet fearful of probing the wound, Jeanne said, quite calmly,

" Mamma, I have had so many things to vex and trouble me for the last few days, I was tired last night, and grieved. Clotilde's farewell, our sudden departure, and Charles's announcement, were too much for me! I behaved like a child, and am ashamed of myself. I was vexed, too, for I knew you would think yourself aggrieved at his having kept silence so long. Of course he was wrong, and he knows it himself. He thought to act for the best, to spare us, but was mistaken. Doubtless he has told you the whole tale. Why he did not immediately upon his return tell us of his marriage, I do not know, save that he and his wife were not happy together; and she wishing to remain at Rome, he was content she should do so. It is very sad, but, mother, his is not a solitary case."

Anxiously Jeanne had watched her mother's darkening brow, and at last she said, with sad sternness,

" And he has lived in the midst of us all these many months, Jeanne, and has kept this secret from me—I who have been al-most a mother to him."

"He was wrong, mother, but there are extenuating circumstances ; he feared for us that the association—that the close intimacy which has ever existed between the Château and the Cottage might suffer. Only be pa-tient and gentle with him now. Remember how you have loved him, with what respect and tenderness he has ever treated you, and so pardon him this, his first, almost his only offence. I think he has suffered much."

"How Charles de Lutz came to marry a woman inferior to himself in birth and edu-cation, astonishes me beyond all things," an-swered Madame. "I could have believed it of any other man sooner than of him."

"And I could have believed it of him

sooner than of most men," replied her
daughter, " because he is the soul of honour
and of truth.   His wife's family considered
Marietta's honour compromised, and insisted
on her entering a convent ; he, to save her
from that death-in-life, married her.   Mother, I think, even while you blame him,
you ought to remember this.   We drove
him to Italy, and we are now bound, for
the honour of our house and name, to receive and stand by his wife, whoever she
may be.   You will receive him well, for
my sake, when he comes, will you not?"
And as she spoke, she threw her arms lovingly round her mother's neck, the softened
look of whose face told her she had gained
the day.   She insisted no longer, and
changing the subject, said,

" I had better go and look after Marie and
the packing. By what train do we leave? "

" By the mid-day or the evening train,"
said Madame—" it depends."

"Then we have no time to lose," answered Jeanne ; and leaving her mother's room,
she crossed the grand salon, when suddenly
Charles de Lutz stood before her. She did
not attempt to avoid him, but remained
quite still in the middle of the room.

" Jeanne, can you pardon me ?" he said.

" Why not ? " she answered, after a
momentary struggle. " If error there
has been, I am as much to blame as
you are, for I have loved you from my
earliest girlhood. Nothing ever came to
break the charm. With you it was different; the thought that I was to be your wife,

while it awakened tenderness, did not—
could not engender love. My mother saw
and felt this. I felt it too, and loving you
so well, how could I bear to be everything,
yet nothing? Had I married you when
you came back from Rome the first time,
Charles, what would your life, and what
would mine have been? You would have
wearied and hankered after what you had
not, and I—I think my heart would have
broken."

"And now, Jeannette?" asked the Count,
sadly.

"Now," she answered, holding out both
her hands towards him—"now we will
take life such as it comes to us—nobly,
bravely, stilling our hearts, hushing our
regrets, living and acting in the present

earnestly and faithfully—you for the wife
you have chosen—I for God and for my
mother."

Her voice trembled as she uttered the
last words, but she still held her head high,
and her eyes were tearless. No word of
reproach that he had not spoken sooner, no
thought that he might have spared her some
part of the present sorrow, seemed to cross
Jeanne's mind. She shivered visibly once—
it was when she remembered he was another
woman's husband ; but that her love was
sin, never came home to her. It was not,
it could not be—her *heart* was pure, and her
love inborn; only it could never be perfected—she must stand alone.

The Count realized their position better.
He knew that stoic calmness could not last ;

he knew the barrier that had arisen between them; he knew how their hearts would beat, and perhaps break from behind the ramparts, let them raise them ever so high. Not now, not yet—this was only the beginning; but in time to come. God help them both!

"Charles," said Jeanne, in the same voice, "where is Marietta now?"

"At Rome—with her father," he answered.

"She must come home—her place is here," was the rejoinder.

"Nay, I think not," replied the Count. "I know Marietta well. She would bring misery on us all. A few months ago I sent Louis to Rome, with a proposal to her father to keep her with him for the present,

I paying her a yearly income sufficient to provide her with every luxury. She herself consented to the arrangement. We are better apart, Jeanne."

"Nay, it cannot, must not be," answered Jeanne. "Your position here is a false one—your marriage must be openly declared, and Marietta must be recognised as "—Jeanne paused and hesitated—it was so hard to give that title to another; then she added softly, "as your wife. She is a foreigner—no one will inquire deeply into her birth; and if she is so beautiful, that and your name will give her her right place in society. The rest will come in time. Grant me this request, cousin. Believe me it will make matters straight, and silence many evil tongues. Remember, she is the mother of your child! She has not sinned against you. Her place is at your side. Fetch her home, Charles."

"Jeanne, Jeanne, you know not what you ask! How would you bear it?—how should I for you?"

A moment's hesitation, then Jeanne answered,

"I am going away, Charles. When I come back, we will begin a new life." She did not look at him again, but continued quietly, "Good-bye. Go to my mother now, and tell her the Countess de Lutz will be here to receive us when we return."

So speaking, she left the room. He did not attempt to follow her—he could not. He knew what those quiet words, that stern outward calm, meant; he felt how

strong was the love and tenderness surging
in his own heart, and how a word, a syllable,
would make the tide overflow. And so he
watched her go—his lost love, his lost happiness; loving her too well to hold her
back.

And she moved slowly away through the
very room she had left lightly a few hours
back, then so full of growing hope and joy,
now so utterly alone. She felt as one be-
numbed with pain. Oh! could she only
have lain down and died! And she knew
that she must live and act! Life seemed
never-ending, the grave where she might
rest at last, so far, so very far away.

In the meantime, left alone, Madame de
Lutz and Miss Ivor looked inquiringly at
each other. They both knew only too well

the question and thought uppermost in their hearts.

"Does she really love him? What brought about this explanation?"

"I never could have believed the Count would have acted thus," was Madame de Lutz's first exclamation, with more of sorrow than of anger in her voice.

"He is not alone to blame," answered Miss Ivor, whose accepted position of friend and counsellor, rather than dependent, authorised her freedom of speech. "When he returned in the Autumn, he openly acknowledged that a mystery enveloped his life; nevertheless you took him home, engaging to ask no questions. He must have some powerful reasons for keeping his wife away from Lutz, and doubtless was convinced he could only do so by letting all the world ignore his marriage. He was wrong, but I cannot believe he was wilfully so; it was an error of judgment, arising, as most of the Count's mistakes do arise, from an over-tenderness, a fear of wounding others."

"And my Jeanne?" said the mother, anxiously.

"Dear Madame," answered Miss Ivor, going up and taking the Countess's hand in hers, "do not deceive yourself any longer. Jeanne has loved her cousin for the last three years. The day she refused to be his wife I found her weeping her heart out in the boudoir, and, girl-like then, she told her love—woman now, she hides it."

"You knew this, and did not tell me!" exclaimed the mother.

"To what purpose?" answered Miss Ivor. "You had refused the Count, Jeanne had done so likewise; you could not, then, call him back, and say you had changed your minds. Human hands had been so busy from early days with this marriage, that I determined, come what might, I would not interfere, but leave it in God's hands. Had I told you Jeanne loved her cousin, you would have been miserable, watching the child's every word and action; she would not have been free to rise above her love, and grow into a noble woman."

"But when he came home you should have told me then," continued Madame.

"I think not," answered Miss Ivor. "Though no word had passed between us, I felt sure Jeanne had been true to her love,

and, I believed, free and unshackled. The
Count could not fail to return it when he
saw her in her ripened beauty. How could
I surmise that other ties bound him ?"

" And now her heart will break," said
Madame. " Why did I thus oppose my
husband's will, deeming myself wiser than
others ?"

The door had opened even while she
spoke, and the Count had entered. As
he did so Miss Ivor left the room. His
face was composed, but very sad. He went
straight up to his aunt, and standing before
her, said,

" You were right, nevertheless, aunt, and
we were all wrong. You, in your woman's
purity, judged marriage to be no idle specu-
lation, no family compact, no momentary

passion—these sooner or later bring misery and degradation. You would not allow me to fall into the first two errors. I have committed the third, and now suffer for it; but, nevertheless, I thank you. You would not do wrong that right might come. I tell you freely now I did not love Jeanne then, though, God pardon me, I worship her now!"

"Charles de Lutz, how dare you speak thus?" exclaimed Madame, her eyes flashing, and her lips trembling with indignation.

"Because I have erred once, and will not do so again," he answered calmly. "Yes, I have told her, aunt, and I tell you now, that I love Jeanne as one never loves save once in a lifetime."

" You told her that, knowing she could not be your wife ?"

" It was my heart and soul that spake, not my reason. I could not be silent. Listen, aunt. Take Jeanne home to England. We cannot kill the love that has grown to its full growth in both our hearts, but we can crush it and keep it down—*we must.* I love so well that I would sooner die than wilfully harm her in word or deed. Why have I kept my wife away from Lutz ?— why have I not announced my marriage? Jeanne has told you, doubtless. Because Marietta is not my equal in rank, and, still worse, in education. But, aunt, you ought to know better. What matters birth or education now-a-days, where there is the gloss of wealth and the *prestige* of such

beauty as Marietta boasts? Nay, it is her
temper, her arrogance, her jealousy, which
has kept me silent. I feared alike for your
peace and my own. Now Jeanne bids me
bring my wife home—she says it is necessary
for my honour and her own. I believe she
is right. This is, therefore, what I propose
doing. While you are in England I will
bring Marietta to Lutz, introduce her in the
county, and then, if you desire it, return for
the Winter to Italy. It will be as well
perhaps for us not to meet for the next year
or two."

"Yes, I think it will be as well," answered Madame, coldly.

"Aunt," said the Count, sadly, "can you
not pardon me? I have sinned truly; but
I am grievously punished too."

"And my Jeanne—how shall I answer to her father for her saddened life?"

The Count paused; then answered, with serious reverence,

"We may not blame the dead, yet I am ofttimes tempted to believe that, could those who have gone before look back upon the deeds and results of their earthly career, they would willingly unlive half their lives on earth. My uncle, by education, and from the effects of example, was led to form projects for Jeanne, not reckoning on counter-influences. Had he left us both free, that which he most desired, and which now has failed, would in all probability have been consummated happily ere this. If the power is granted him now to look down on earth, believe me, aunt, he sees and judges

events very differently from what he did
when, a dying, anxious man, he feared to
leave his child in God's hands, and strove
with his finite judgment to regulate her
future. His errors have been pardoned
him ; we trust he will not be less merciful
to you and me. And Jeanne—our good,
our gentle Jeanne—I cannot cease to love
her, aunt—as soon bid me cease to breathe
the fresh, free air of heaven, yet live ; but
from henceforth my task shall be to smoothe
her path, to stand aside and let her pass ;
never by word or deed to rouse into being
hopes and thoughts that may not be. It is
a hard task, but where there is will and
strength, surely there is also power."

"God grant it, Charles de Lutz !" said
Madame, doubtfully ; " you speak bravely,

and you mean truly, I know, but, alas! eyes will speak, hands will meet, and love is strong—stronger than death. You have done a grievous wrong."

" I know it, aunt—farewell !" and slowly he moved towards the door.

She saw him go regretfully, for he had been almost a son to her; still, she would not stay his steps—she was angered for Jeanne's sake. Thus had they parted, save that the opposite door opened, giving admittance to Jeanne herself. Anxiously she looked from one to the other, a pained, troubled expression gradually overspreading her face.

" You are going, Charles ?" she said, after a minute. He bowed his head in token of assent ; then she went up to him,

and holding out her hand, said gently—
"Good-bye, my cousin. When next we
meet, remember we shall expect to welcome the Countess Charles de Lutz. Mother, you are parting friends, surely?" and
still holding the Count's hand, she half
drew him towards Madame. "I have had
pain enough to-day," she said, in a low
tone—"do not make it greater!"

"God knows I would not, Jeanne," answered the Count, sadly, holding out his
hand to the angered Countess; and Jeanne,
taking her mother's, laid it in his palm.

"Mother, for my sake," she pleaded.

"Let it be so, then," answered the Countess, bursting into tears. "For her sake I
forgive you, Charles de Lutz."

And as the Count bent his head, she

kissed him on the brow. He waited not to hear another word, fearful lest his own emotion should overpower him. Without even looking at Jeanne, with hasty steps he left the room.

"Thank you, mother," was all Jeanne said; and, moving about quietly, she gathered various little knicknacks together, until she saw that Madame de Lutz had somewhat recovered her composure. Then she spoke of the hour, of various things that had to be arranged; and was so entirely herself that Madame began gradually to lose her fear, and to think that perhaps, after all, she had exaggerated the evil.

That night they left the Cottage, and proceeded on their road to England, ignorant of the fact that the Count de Lutz accom-

panied them the whole way as far as Calais.
He must watch over Jeanne awhile longer;
he could not let her go thus alone! From
a distance, in secret, henceforth, he must
follow her; but none the less faithfully,
none the less truly. As long as she was in
sight, he watched the vessel that bore away
all that was brightest, purest in his life.
Then, when it had quite disappeared beyond
the horizon, he turned homewards, looking
stern duty steadily in the face, determined
not to shrink henceforth from it, let it come
in what form it might.

And Jeanne, speeding through the green
fields of England, gazed for the first time
on her mother's land. Rich and fair it
seemed to her, with villages dotted here
and there; church spires rising upwards to

the sky, as if to sanctify the land; tranquillity, wealth, and peace everywhere. And she was fain to ask herself if, in those ancestral homes lying imbedded amidst those ancient trees, if beneath those thatched cottage roofs, with their smiling gardens, there could be many hearts struggling, loving, aching, as hers did?

In London they were met by Gordon, whose account of his father was such as to determine Madame de Lutz to continue her journey without further delay. The Reverend James Elliot had begun life a poor man. One of a large family, he knew that, once his education completed, he had nothing more, in a pecuniary sense, to expect from his parents. Whatever remained at their death, must naturally go to his sisters.

From choice, and because he felt it to be his own especial mission, he had entered the Church, and for some years had worked hard in one of the worst London parishes. Gradually, year by year, the brothers and sisters of that once united household had been laid to their rest, until at last only two remained, Mary and James Elliot. They lived together in their modest home, cheering and comforting each other, until the brother one day brought home a wife, a noble-hearted, generous woman, who made the lonely sister thoroughly and completely welcome in her home.

Shortly previous to his marriage, James Elliot had been presented with a living in Wiltshire; and from henceforth his difficulties were removed. In his country home

plenty and peace awaited him. The following year Mary Elliot married the Count De
Lutz, and only once since had brother and
sister met, though they had ever maintained
an affectionate and frequent correspondence.
That once had been on the occasion of his
wife's death, when Gordon was about twelve
years old. Several children had been born
to the Vicar, but with the exception of the
eldest they had all died in infancy; and at
last the wife and mother followed, and was
laid in the peaceful churchyard beside her
babes. Mr. Elliot had never really recovered
the shock of her death; his was one of those
sensitive natures which cannot throw off
sorrow, and which clings as tenaciously to a
lost as to a living love. All his energy, all
his ambition, was from henceforth concen-

trated on his only son. No expense was
spared to give him a first-rate education—Eton, the University, foreign travel
—nothing was denied him, and his career
promised thus far to be a brilliant success. He had chosen the law as a profes-
sion, and his talents were already highly
spoken of.

He was keeping his second term when his
father, who had been somewhat ailing for
the last few months, was suddenly laid low
by a stroke of paralysis. Then it was that
the earnest desire to see his only remaining
sister came to the dying man. It is strange,
but nevertheless true, that when life is ebb-
ing away one returns in spirit to the days of
one's childhood, retracing step by step each
incident in life's journey. Vividly the memory

of early friends arises—of brothers and sisters long since gone to their rest; and the craving to feel once more the touch of long-forgotten hands grows painfully strong. And so Gordon had sent for his aunt; and with feverish impatience James Elliot awaited her arrival. They met at last, not without sadness; how could it be otherwise?—they who had parted in the full strength of life and health—and now!

But Mr. Elliot, in his long life of preaching to others, had not failed to learn for himself the true lesson of Christianity. He knew the time was close at hand when he must bid farewell to the world and worldly things; and from the moment his dimmed eyes met the tearful gaze of his dearly-loved sister, he was content, his soul was satisfied;

he could have exclaimed with Simeon of old, "Lord, now lettest thou thy servant depart in peace." After the first day or two the Vicarage resumed its usual aspect of quiet cheerfulness; no one could have imagined that beneath that roof a human soul awaited from hour to hour its great, its final call.

Jeanne had never seen her uncle since her early childhood. Her remembrance of him was therefore very vague, and he would certainly not have recognized, in the fair, graceful girl, the merry, romping child of twelve years back. There is a strange affinity in sorrow, and, from the first hour of their meeting, uncle and niece felt drawn towards each other. There was a charm for Jeanne in that calm, noble face, with its soft white hair, brushed back from the marble brow! That almost motionless figure seemed to soothe her impatience; and the dying man, with the acute instincts of the dying, looking into her face, saw there what others in life and health seemed to ignore, namely, a struggle of the soul, a sort of life agony; he, going to his rest, pitied the young soldier just entering the battle-field, and seeing her so frail, marvelled how she would demean herself; while Jeanne, on her side, almost envied him the battle fought, and nearly over.

Pleasant and home-like was that country Vicarage. A long, low building, stretching in front of a well-kept lawn, bestudded with standard rose-trees and bright flower-beds. It consisted actually of two buildings, the old and the new. To the former belonged the library and dining-room, both somewhat low and dark, with small Gothic, pointed windows; then came the projecting porch, covered with climbing plants—the yellow bankshire rose and honeysuckle intermingled —on the other side of which ran the large new drawing-room, which Mr. Elliot had built to please his wife, and furnished with elegant comfort. Alas! ere the gloss had worn off the pretty chintz and many-flowered carpet, the mistress was sleeping her last sleep in the churchyard yonder; and from henceforth the new drawing-room was rarely used, save for a chance guest, who was not considered intimate enough to be introduced into the Vicar's private sanctum.

But these occasions grew more and more rare, and, after his illness, ceased altogether. When he could leave his own room he was rolled into the library, and remained there the livelong day. So, though the drawing-room had been duly aired and put in order, in anticipation of Madame de Lutz's arrival, it was scarcely more frequented than before, both mother and daughter showing a marked preference for the somewhat sombre, yet quaint and home-like, library, with its shelves of books, great ecclesiastical volumes, ancient pictures of celebrated divines looking down grimly on the occupants, so passionless, so calm, one inwardly wondered if they ever moved, and felt, and acted as living men.

CHAPTER XII.

TWO or three evenings after their arrival the whole family was assembled in this same library—Mr. Elliot, in his large easy-chair, watching each in turn, Madame working beside him, Gordon reading, and Jeanne leaning listlessly against the framework of the open lattice window; for although the lamp was lit, the warm, early Summer air was pleasant. Listlessly, I said, Jeanne stood, her white dress scarcely less colourless than her face. A sort of grey, shadowy look seemed to hang over her; she was doing nothing, seeing nothing, though her eyes were fixed upon the flowery lawn. Her soul was far away, living over again the hour when she had seen the pitiless barrier arise which must for ever separate her fate from him she loved. Standing thus, it seemed as if she still felt his kiss upon her lips, and heard his gentle words breathing mingled love and pain.

Gradually—very gradually—Jeanne was learning to realize her position. Alone— from henceforth ever alone! The idea that another could fill her heart never presented itself to her; her heart was full—full to overflowing. There was no vacant place in it.

"Gordon," said Mr. Elliot, suddenly breaking the silence, "couldn't you go into Salisbury to-morrow, and see if Barret has not a couple of decent saddle-horses? A good gallop over our downs would help to bring the colour into Jeanne's pale cheeks."

"Oh! uncle, you are very good! I am quite well. My pale cheeks are no criterion of ill-health—I am always pale."

"Then we must try and see what English air can do for you," he answered, smiling. "Gordon, do you think it possible to find a safe lady's horse?"

"Quite possible, sir. I will go over the first thing to-morrow morning."

"Do so, and let us see how well you can do the honours of Wiltshire."

"Indeed, uncle, you are too kind," said Jeanne, going up to him, and stooping over his chair, she kissed him in token of gratitude.

"Too kind, Jeanne, one cannot be in this world," answered the invalid; and drawing her towards him, he continued, in a voice so low as only to reach her ears—"Remember, child, there is an end to every sorrow. Patience, Jeanne; life is only dawning for you."

The girl drew back, startled and pained. How had she thus betrayed herself that even a comparative stranger had become master of her secret?

That night, for the first time since her love had been so rudely nipped in the bud, Jeanne, laying herself down on her bed, wet her pillow with tears—not bitter tears; no anger, no jealousy found place in her heart; they flowed as the blood flows from the wounds of the untended, uncared-for soldier on the battle-field. Since she had left Lutz, she had lived like one walking in her sleep; but it was a restless, wearying sleep. Never for one moment had she been unconscious—never for one moment had her soul been lightened of its pain. Night after night she had lain with her eyes wide open, not thinking, not dreaming— simply counting the hours as they passed, and existing. Now the flood-gates were opened, and moaning in her agony, Jeanne lay, until, towards morning, wearied out, she rose, and throwing open the window, let the cool air blow upon her heated brow.

Day was just breaking. The stars had faded from the sky, all save one, which, as Jeanne lifted her heavy eyes, shone down upon her from its place above the ivy-grown church-tower. Its clear, silvery light, piercing to her troubled heart, seemed to say,

"Peace, peace, child! From everlasting I have looked down on sorrows such as thine. Learn thou to look upwards, to pierce beyond the skies, to tell all your sorrow, all your love, to that Christ who is so pitiful, so tender. Fearest thou men—their misconstruction, their unkindness? Him thou needst not fear. Thy weaknesses are known, thy struggles are appreciated. He will comfort thee in thy despair, and strengthen thee in thy feebleness."

And standing at that open window, Jeanne prayed. Floating across her mind there came the remembrance of her last conversation with Clotilde, in which she had de-

clared so proudly that she asked not to be
exempted from the trials and temptations
of this world, only to be kept " unspotted,"
and now, at the very outset, should she
shrink away? Nay, that were impossible!
Within those convent walls, far away in that
fair land of France, she knew that one was
praying for her night and day; surely
thus wrestling together against evil, they
might conquer fate. And the dew of comfort
penetrated the young girl's heart, refreshing
and soothing her; and when the first rays
of the morning sun overpowered and hid
from view the little star, her gentle com-
forter, she turned back into her room, and
lying down on her bed, fell into a deep
slumber.

Her mother, coming in to look at her a

few hours later, and seeing her pale and weary, had not the heart to wake her, and so let her sleep on. She knew her child was struggling and suffering; but she dared not probe the wound. Sometimes she was tempted to do so, but Jeanne was outwardly so composed, so still, she never gave her the opportunity; and so Madame waited, and hoped that all might yet be well.

When, thus refreshed, Jeanne once more joined the family circle, her uncle, looking in her face, saw that a change had come over her. It was as if a cloud had burst, and a ray of sunshine had become visible. She fell so easily into the habits and ways of life at the Vicarage, that one would have thought she had ever been a daughter of the house. Mr. Elliot succumbed at once to the

charm of her presence. Her tender care of
him, her delicate attentions, and, above all,
her clear intelligence and power of sympathy, rendered her invaluable to him as a
companion, and soon he could not bear her
out of his sight for any length of time. Still,
every afternoon he insisted on her taking
long rides over the country with Gordon,
and would have his invalid chair rolled to
the open window to see her mount, declar-
ing he could never have believed a French
girl could sit a horse so well. He thought
to tease her by calling her "a French girl,"
but Jeanne retorted quickly, with flushed
cheeks,

"Nay, uncle, if French girls were brought
up as English girls are, I am not sure but

what they would carry off the palm in more ways than one."

And though Mr. Elliot poo-pooed the idea, he could not but think, looking at his niece, that the exquisite grace and courtesy, the vivacity and ready wit, the simplicity yet perfect taste of her dress, were very charming, and would add not a little to the value of those sterling qualities which unmistakably adorn an English girl, but which are often hidden beneath a rough uncouthness and want of tact which mar what is of itself intrinsically beautiful.

And so days and weeks passed calmly by, and Jeanne rested in her English home. Often, often she looked back, in after-times, to this period of her existence as given her by God to gather up her strength for the combat. Here for a time we will leave her, and see what is passing at the Château de Lutz.

CHAPTER XIII.

FOR a few weeks after the inhabitants of the Cottage had left, the Count still remained at the Château, not inactive, for he caused the long shut-up apartments to be opened, and sent for workmen from Paris, who began rapidly to effect various alterations and improvements; for the Count knew and appreciated the necessity of receiving the Countess with all due honour. When the neighbourhood became aware of what was taking place at the Château, curiosity was aroused to the highest pitch. The

Count was at last about to enter into
the estate of matrimony, and of course
Mademoiselle Jeanne was the future Countess. There was no divided opinion on that
point.

It was not long before Charles de Lutz
heard these rumours, and at once he determined to silence them. Assembling his
principal tenants, he informed them quietly
that he had been married for the last two
years; that his wife was an Italian lady,
who, through severe illness, had been prevented up to the present from joining him in
France. They knew how near to death he
himself had been, and that he had returned
amongst them simply to arrange his affairs.
He had been spared, and his wife also had
so far recovered her health that, as soon as

the Château was ready to receive its new mistress, he should fetch her from her father's home to his.

Such was the only explanation he vouchsafed. He received the customary congratulations with courteous *sang-froid*, and there the matter dropped. People talked and wondered for a few days, delighted to imagine there might be ground for scandal. A vast number of suppositions were made, an unlimited amount of stories told, all alike without the shadow of foundation ; but as no one took the trouble to contradict or to verify them, they one by one fell to the ground, and people became content to await the arrival of the new Countess, before they pronounced an opinion upon her.

On the estate, however, there was a cer-

tain feeling of disappointment and regret.
Jeanne was so well beloved, they could ill
brook another Countess. When the news
first reached the Marquise de la Croix, she
was for a moment stunned. This, then, was
the secret she had been unable to solve.
Quickly she reviewed her position, and came
to the conclusion that at last it was pro-
pitious to her desires. Besides love for the
Count, another passion now occupied no insig-
nificant place in her heart—namely, hatred
for Jeanne. The girl had despised, had ventured to reprove her—*that* she could never
pardon ; and, moreover, she felt instinctively
that, married or not, there was still a link between the Count and Jeanne, which roused
her utmost jealousy. One thing was evident to her—let the new Countess be who

or what she might, she could not hold any very powerful grasp on the Count's heart, for him to remain nearly a year quietly at Lutz, while she was in Italy. It seemed to her that with a little tact and flattery she might easily initiate herself into favour. A foreigner, a stranger, would be thankful to anyone who would stand by, support and help her. Once a footing gained in the Count's household, she knew it would be no easy matter to oust her again. So she would wait patiently, see where the weak point in the fortress lay, make the breach, and enter. Such was her plan.

The Count, on his arrival at Rome, found his wife absent—she had gone to Sorrento with her father for the Summer months. Thither he followed her. Marietta did not expect her husband, and was but half pleased when he presented himself before her. The violent, passionate love she had once borne him had long since died out, as all love not based on something better than mere passion must do sooner or later. She had grown accustomed to the easy life of luxurious idleness which the ample income her husband provided enabled her to maintain. The freedom, too, was agreeable. Her great beauty now ripened into perfection, attracted admirers, whom, without passing the bounds of propriety, she allowed to hover round her. Naturally her position was a difficult one ; and, be it said to her honour, no breath of scandal had attached itself to her name.

Madame Lutz (for Marietta had never

known either her husband's title or the position he held in his own country, otherwise she had not been content to remain in the background) was admired wherever she went; and people wondered at her husband leaving so young and beautiful a wife to her own devices. For Marietta, now in her convalescence, would by many have been considered far more attractive than formerly. Her beauty had matured, as Italian women's do rapidly. There was no longer the shadow of the girl about her— she was a fully developed, magnificent woman, looking more than her age, stately and dignified in every movement. Her husband was somewhat surprised at the change he found both in her manner and appearance. He did not deceive himself—he knew that her passion for him had died out, but he knew, too, she would be even more jealous, more *exigeante* than formerly, if that were possible. The form, now for the substance.

So husband and wife met, with an outside show of pleasure; but the one with a lazy annoyance at being disturbed in an easy mode of existence, and the other with a determination to perform a duty which he felt to be burdensome, and the result of which he feared.

There is something strange and ineffably sad in the meeting of two persons who, to all intents and purposes, have once loved each other, and have now ceased to do so. The Count felt this acutely, though Marietta could scarcely do so. With her all was instinct—she loved, and she ceased to love; she desired, and she ceased to desire.

The evening after the Count's arrival, the two strolled out together towards the sea. It was a lovely Italian night; the air soft and balmy, impregnated with the fresh sea breeze.

"After all," thought Charles de Lutz, "Marietta is quiet and happy here. Why should I seek to change her life?"

The answer came. "She is your wife. Her place is at your side. In duty you are bound to her, and she to you."

And the Count, standing on the sea-shore, recognised the truth, and, turning to his wife, said gently,

"Marietta, do you know I have come to take you to my home in France?"

"Ah!" she said, her brow clouding over. "We are well here. Why cannot we remain in Italy?"

"Because, Marietta, we have duties to perform in France which we may not ignore. In giving you my name, I imposed them upon you. I knew that, unused to them, they would appear both hard and difficult; and so I hid them from you, hoping that time and custom would render them less irksome. But now it is imperative that you should assume your real position. You are not simply Madame Lutz, but Madame la Comtesse de Lutz, the wife of one of the richest men in France, and belonging to one of the oldest and most honoured families. Marietta, it is no light task that lies before you—the Countesses de Lutz have ever been beloved and honoured by the peasants who tilled their lands, and the nobles who bowed in courteous homage before them."

"A Countess!—am I a real Countess?" exclaimed Marietta, looking up in bewildered astonishment.

"Yes—a real Countess, Marietta," said her husband, smiling.

A lightning flash of pleasure shot over Marietta's face, but died out instantly, as she answered quickly,

"If I am a Countess, I ought to have a castle, diamonds, jewels. Why have I not had all this for these last three years that I have been your wife?"

"Because," he answered firmly, "you were unprepared for, uneducated to your position. A simple artist's daughter, shut out as you had been from the world, you could with difficulty have assumed at once the cares and responsibilities of rank and wealth. I thought to raise you gently to your throne, Marietta."

" You have deceived and robbed me of my rights," she answered doggedly.

" Do you think so ?" answered the Count, quite calmly. "Still, in reality you have been no loser. I have denied you nothing. All the luxuries that wealth can give you have enjoyed. You married me as simply Monsieur de Lutz, the artist. I was no Count to you in those days; and had we really loved and understood each other, I think we should have been happier with our simple artist's name than we ever shall be now as Count and Countess de Lutz. But this is no time for recriminations. Let us begin life anew," he continued. "Never fear, Marietta, the Castle has not run away, but is in due preparation for the reception of its mistress. Jewels and diamonds, and all that you covet, shall be yours; and, in truth, no Countess de Lutz in the past will ever have graced them better."

Pleased with the compliment, flattered by the prospect of her future grandeur, Marietta's good-humour rapidly returned, and taking her husband's arm, they re-commenced their walk along the shore, while she eagerly launched into every possible inquiry concerning their future home, their wealth and position. And the Count was contented to gratify her whim. From henceforth his course was clear—to satisfy, to make her happy, and thus to keep in check the undisciplined passions of her nature.

When they once more reached home, and Marietta had informed her father of her new position, and her intention of following her husband to France, a new difficulty arose. Signor Rocco had grown accustomed to the easy life he had of late led with his daughter, and looked forward with marked dissatisfaction to once more depending on his own exertions. He therefore at once intimated his intention of following his child into her new country. But against this the Count stood firm. He knew he should have a difficult task with Marietta, and he determined it should not be rendered more so by her father's presence. So he at once told the Signor that from henceforth he might consider him as his banker; that a yearly income would be settled upon him, his debts paid, and a certain sum given him for present outlay. This generosity so overcame the Signor, that he was ready to go or to remain wherever the Count desired; and as it was especially stipulated that he should remain in Italy, the idea of following Marietta fell to the ground.

The Count and Countess lingered a few days longer at Sorrento, and then went to Rome to make their final preparations. Marietta hurried everything on. She was impatient to assume her rank; she considered herself as a queen long kept out of her kingdom, and who is in haste to reign. Not so Charles de Lutz. He was in no hurry to return. He looked things steadily in the face, and saw the difficulties of his position. Still he knew there was nothing left but do go straight forward. Marietta in society at Amonville would pass muster —he no longer feared that; her beauty and his name would steer her safely through that by no means intricate labyrinth. He doubted not that in time she might even become the fashion. Anything peculiar in her manners would be put down to her foreign education. She would be something new—an excitement, a novelty.

Only she must not ruffle his aunt's and Jeanne's life. That he must guard against at every hazard. He therefore spoke to Marietta of the only two beings left in his home. He told her how his aunt had brought him up, and how he, in his turn, had acted as Jeanne's guardian.

"And was it after this cousin you called our little child?" asked Marietta.

"Yes," answered the Count. "It was a pleasant, familiar name to me; now it is sacred!"

"How old is Jeanne, and is she beautiful?" asked Marietta.

"She must be a little younger than you, just about twenty," answered the Count. "You ask if she is beautiful. I scarcely think so. Strangers do not say so, and, as for me, I am no judge. Her face has always been familiar to me. It is very sweet —that is all I can tell you, Marietta. And Jeanne is good and gentle. I desire nothing so much as that perfect union should exist

between the Château and the Cottage. You
will strive to maintain it, will you not?"

"Why should I do otherwise," she answered, sharply, "if they do not interfere
with me? I shall be the real Countess,
shall I not?"

"Yes," said Charles, "you will be the
reigning Countess—the mistress of the Château—if that is what you mean, Marietta."

"Then it is well," was the answer; and
Marietta drew herself up with dignity and
proud satisfaction. "If they keep their
place, I shall keep mine. A Countess!—
who ever thought of plain Marietta Rocco,
the artist's daughter, becoming a Countess!"

Her husband smiled at her childish delight
and wonder, but the smile was succeeded
by a sigh, as involuntarily he thought of one

who would have cared so little for the title of " Countess," could she have borne that of " wife."

About the time of his return, he received two or three letters from his aunt, in all of which her intention of prolonging her stay in England grew more and more evident.

" My brother's health," she wrote in one, " does not improve. It would be almost ‑cruel to leave him now. Besides, he has grown so attached to Jeanne, that I think the pain of parting from her would be very injurious to him ; the least shock or worry to his nervous system would doubtless bring on another and a fatal attack. We shall therefore remain here, unless something especial should recall us to Lutz. If the Winter is mild, we may not return till the

Spring; but that will depend upon Jeanne's health. If she can stand the English climate, I should prefer wintering here—you understand why; if forced to return, I shall, of course, unhesitatingly do so."

Silently he read and sadly recognised the barrier rising higher and higher between him and Jeanne. He closed his eyes to shut out her image, but clear and distinct she stood before him in her bright girlhood, in her gentle womanhood; only when, in his wild longing, he stretched out his hands towards her, she faded from his sight. She was to him like the running streams of pure limpid water which the thirsty traveller in the desert dreams he sees, but which he may not taste of—may not realize. On through the Sahara he must go, with the glittering, golden sand beneath his feet, and the burning sun pouring down upon him without mercy, glorying in its power, while he faints for thirst.

At last they started homewards, Marietta, in high good temper, curious and excited. They travelled rapidly, and at their last resting-place having taken a night-train, arrived with early morning at Amonville. A carriage was awaiting them, and so they drove at once out to Lutz. It was a fresh, bright morning early in September; there was a ruddy tint over the woods; the leaves from the great forest trees had scarcely begun to fall, but their hue had changed from green to a rich yellowish red, as if the sun, in bidding them farewell, had stooped and kissed them lingeringly, and so left his shadow behind. The scene had a sort of strengthening, renovating effect on Charles de Lutz. A tender feeling crept into his heart for the wife he was bringing home. So young and beautiful! He did not deceive himself; he knew how essentially selfish Marietta was; but, after all, that might be the effect of climate and of education. The entire change might work wonders—the force of home influence, the power of example—who could tell, they might be happy even yet?

I have said once before, in the early part of my story, that Charles de Lutz, notwithstanding the mistakes and errors of his life, was a good man; therefore he was merciful, and always inclined to look on the bright rather than the dark side of human nature.

And so his courage and his hopes rose high as he crossed the boundary of his ancestral home. They were young, and time was all-powerful; he would do his duty to his young wife, and surely a blessing would follow. And Jeanne?—she might be happy too. Another man's wife—Gordon Elliot's, per-haps! A great pain shot across his heart at the thought; and, raising his hat, he passed his hand across his brow, as if to dispel an evil vision. At the same moment the carriage swept past the first outpost on the Lutz estate. Turning to his wife, he took her hand, saying,

"Marietta, welcome to Lutz; we are on our own lands now."

"Where is the Château?" she asked, eagerly.

"You will not see it for a quarter of an hour yet; it is embedded in trees," he answered.

"You did not tell me the estate was so large," replied the new Countess. "Is all we see from here your property?" she asked, with evident pride.

"Not quite," he answered, "all on the right hand belongs to the Château; but out yonder to the left Jeanne's land begins. Formerly, you know, it was but one estate, and is now only separated by the high road; in some parts, indeed, the vineyards touch each other."

"Then Mademoiselle Jeanne is as rich as you are!" said Marietta.

"Not quite," answered her husband, "though she ought to have been. During

my minority, while my uncle kept a strict
eye and hand over my property, he was less
particular about his own affairs, and not
thinking he should ever marry, was somewhat careless as to his expenditure. Then
there is my aunt's third out of the estate.
So Jeanne, though well off, is not so wealthy
as she might have been."

"Who manages her estate?" asked Marietta.

"Her man of business and myself. You
know, I told you I was her guardian."

"Strange they never thought of marrying
you, and making the two estates one; it
would have been only natural," said Marietta.

"My aunt is an English woman, and in
her country marriages of interest are not

looked on with a favourable eye," answered the Count.

"So," said Marietta, thoughtfully. At the same moment the carriage stopped at the lodge gates.

"Will you get out here and walk up to the house?" said the Count; " you will see the Château better."

Marietta assented ; and, alighting, they proceeded leisurely on foot up the long avenue of stately trees, until the Château in all its grandeur broke upon them. Then they paused, and Marietta looked half wonderingly upon her future home. There it stood, with all its noble façade, flanked on either side by turrets; its long terrace walk, with the double row of linden trees, and sloping down the soft green lawn, the pride of all the country round, which had been made under Madame's orders. A real English lawn, smooth as velvet, with its border of many-coloured flowers and rich shrubbery, out of the midst of which rose the tall gynerium, now in its full glory, with its white wavy plumes nodding in majestic pride. Yes, it was something to find one's self thus suddenly the mistress of such a home.

"*Come è bella!*" said Marietta, holding up her hands in admiration.

"Yes," said Charles de Lutz, with earnest pride; "the Château de Lutz has always been noted for its beauty. God grant, Marietta, that we may find rest and happiness beneath its roof!"

"Why not?" she answered hastily—"why not?" But she spoke carelessly, not troubling herself to think from whence true happiness springs and flourishes, ignoring that it needed tender nurture and great care. Seeing only the grandeur and wealth of her new position, she deemed that these could suffice, for ambition and pride had taken the place of love in her heart, and were now her ruling passions. Triumphantly leaning on her husband's arm, she entered the Château, and passed through the great hall, where the servants and chief tenants had assembled to greet their new mistress. Cordially Charles de Lutz spoke to each as he presented to them his wife. A loud murmur of admiration arose as Marietta threw back her veil, and one and all, even the least skilled in the appreciation of beauty, became aware of the strange, marvellous

loveliness of the new Countess. They had neither been prepared nor inclined to receive
Marietta with alacrity, angered as they were
that any one else should occupy the place
they had so long associated with Jeanne; but
now, in one second, they forgot their pre-
judices, they forgot gentle, simple Jeanne,
with her almost child-like grace. Fascinated,
charmed, they looked upon the beautiful
woman before them, and proudly accepted
her as worthy of their master's choice.

"Vivent le Comte et la Comtesse de
Lutz!" broke simultaneously from each and
all.

With stately grace, Marietta bowed her
thanks, saying in her soft Italian, " *Grazie!*
grazie!"

Then her husband led her through the

grand salons, to that wing of the Château which had been prepared for her. Throwing open the door, he said,

" Marietta, these are your own rooms—your own especial sanctum."

So saying, they entered, and Marietta gazed around in bewildered admiration. The apartment consisted of three rooms—boudoir, bedroom, and dressing-room, opening one into the other, and each furnished for its own peculiar use. Nothing had been forgotten, nothing neglected, all that wealth and taste could do to make a new abode pleasant and beautiful had been done. Everything was in its place. The eye rested everywhere on richly-sculptured wood, soft-coloured satins, and thick carpets, half covering the polished oak floors.

Loud were Teresa's exclamations of delight as she followed her mistress. Silently Marietta looked around her, but no word escaped her lips, until, leaving her husband's arm, she threw herself languidly on the sofa, saying,

"I cannot imagine why you did not bring me here sooner. This is better—much better even than Italy."

"I am glad you are pleased with your home, Marietta," was the Count's only answer.

A cold, strange feeling of isolation was creeping over him—he looked at the beautiful woman beside him, and asked himself if he were not dreaming? Was all love gone out between them? Must they live henceforth together without any deeper feeling coming to hallow and sweeten their existences than that of mutual interest? It could not, must not be!

Rousing himself, he went up to his wife, and speaking a few tender words of welcome, kissed her brow. She hardly seemed to hear or see him, for, rising, she proceeded to examine the rooms in detail. Ignorant of the use of many of the objects she saw, at every moment she applied to him for explanations, and he gave them gently and patiently, as he would have done to a child, until, wearied out, Marietta declared she would lie down and rest. Then her husband left her, and bent his steps towards his own studio, which, in accordance with his orders, had remained unchanged. Throwing himself into the nearest chair, and leaning his head upon his hands, he fell into deep thought. It was not perhaps the wisest thing for him to do, especially in that room, where everything spoke so eloquently of the last hour he had spent with Jeanne. But we are not always wise, and in moments of weakness, insensibly our strength and wisdom fail us.

It were useless to try to describe what his feelings were at this time; sad and regretful they could not fail to be. Unfaithful to his wife, dishonouring to Jeanne—that they never were. Bound to one woman, he knew he loved another, yet he recognized the fact that in fulfilling his duty to one he fulfilled it virtually to both; and he never swerved in his determination not to pass the line—narrow though it might be, and was—which lay between actual right and wrong.

END OF THE SECOND VOLUME.

LONDON : PRINTED BY MACDONALD AND TUGWELL, BLENHEIM HOUSE.

www.ingramcontent.com/pod-product-compliance
Lightning Source LLC
Chambersburg PA
CBHW021217270326

41929CB00010B/1170